Sensitive Matters

If it is sensitive, it matters

Tim Naden

Contents

Foreword

What if I told you debt collection was the most cut-throat, morally bankrupt, wildly entertaining profession you've never understood?

Forget everything you think you know about banks, business, or what happens when you miss a payment. This book rips the lid off the fluorescent-lit trenches of modern finance and shows you a world where empathy is optional, caffeine is currency, and repossessing a Mercedes from a daycare drop-off is just another Tuesday.

Inside, you'll meet Sam Crews, a man torn between ethics and ego, invoices and ideals who leads a team of collectors so savage, so sharp, they make bounty hunters look like babysitters. And just when you think it's all about the money, in walks sensitivity training. Spoiler alert: they're not ready.

It's gritty. It's hilarious. It's shockingly human.

And yes, someone really does say, "Sell to anyone with a pulse."

If you've ever wanted to know what it feels like to run headfirst into the corporate sausage factory, this book hands you the goggles and throws you in.

Buckle up. Sign here. And whatever you do, don't miss a payment.

Chapter 1 Cash or Keys

"It's good news for the Blues

Now, there's no more time to lose

Cos we're hot on the trail

And there's no way we're gonna fail

So get your coat on and get moving

Cos we don't know the meaning of losing

So come on, come on

Get down to Goodison Park

Wooooo.

Everton, we never shone so brightly.

Everton, the spirit of The Blues."

https://www.youtube.com/watch?v=OEekoV4en-g

The sound of the 6 a.m. alarm, the team song, "Spirit Of The Blues," of the English Premier

League (EPL) football club, Everton, awakens Sam Crews from his slumber, alone on his expansive queen-sized bed. It's hard to know what Sam loves more - the Everton team or the Everton song.

Consequently he does not turn off the alarm, rather letting the song boom for the next three minutes.

Sam promptly jumps to his feet and darts straight to the top drawer of a tallboy next to the bed, upon which is a framed photo of his favourite Everton player, Tim Cahill, which he opens revealing an array of socks and underwear from which Sam plucks a pair of each. Also inside is a small box containing an engagement ring, at which Sam glances before closing the drawer.

The morning light crept through the blinds as he moved towards the shower. Here, within the steam and solitude, was where Sam, an imposing figure. 6'2", in his late twenties, with an athletic and muscular physique and a thick crop of dark brown hair, is at his most ponderous and creative, where both body and mind are cleansed. Sam likes to refer to himself as "Sam the ideas man" and the shower is often from where his ideas emerge. On the weekend, his thoughts range from a song he is writing to playing soccer to where he will go out on a Saturday night. But during the working week, his mind is firmly on his team: Car Loans Collections of Global Bank. Sam never saw himself working in finance, he'd always dreamt of becoming a writer and making a life, not just career, out of words with vast riches to flow his way. He was particularly inspired by journalists who became authors and pictured himself in a similar vein. After completing a journalism degree at 22 years of age he was immediately offered a cadetship in Sydney's number 1 masthead and a career in his love for words was now realised.

Then came the wake-up call. The long hours, the low pay, the endless hustle. Conversations with senior journalists crushed his illusions. The truth was stark: years of grind for little financial reward. The strain extended beyond the newsroom; his three-year relationship with Abbey frayed. By twenty-four he was a father to Vincent, a child for whom he hadn't planned nor initially wanted. The engagement ring had been meant for Abbey but their lives had taken a different course. When Vincent was born, Sam withdrew, choosing the camaraderie of his newsroom over the responsibilities of fatherhood. When Abbey finally had enough he hadn't fought to stay.

A year later, he made another choice—words or money? He chose money.

The advertisement read: Debt Collection Associate—
Base Salary + Commission. It wasn't glamorous, but it
promised control over his earnings. He joined
Australian Credit Consolidation (ACC), where he
learned the art of negotiation, the psychology of
debtors, and the rules of leverage.

He excelled, thriving on the challenge of persuading
people to pay.

Eighteen months later, he outgrew ACC and moved to
Global Bank. Within six months, he led a team of ten
collectors, turning them into the company's top
performers. The money was good. The work was
ruthless. But Sam didn't dwell on ethics. Success was
measured in numbers, and his team was winning.

Sam's shower was relatively short, having mentally
prepared and mapped out the day ahead.

Dressed in a collared shirt, chino trousers, and a blazer,
he headed to the train station. Travel to and from work
is a two-step affair involving both train and ferry. While
Global Bank's main office is in the Sydney Central
Business District (CBD), the Collections arm is based
in Manly, a beachside suburb in Sydney's north. Trains

do not operate in this area with public transport in the form of buses and ferries:

Sam always opts for the latter.

The twenty-minute train ride was predictable. He timed it perfectly to step straight onto the scheduled ferry, avoiding unnecessary waiting. Despite the daily repetition, he still savoured the ride - the sea air, the open water, and the relaxed atmosphere.

Arriving in Manly, he walked briskly towards the office, cutting through The Corso, a bustling pedestrian mall lined with surf shops, pubs, and cafés.

There is one particular spot Sam favours, metres away from the popular Staines Hotel, which is "reserved" for buskers and broadly known as the "Buskers Burrow," though the performers themselves simply call it The Burrow. On this occasion, Paddy Roach, a good friend of Sam, is in The Burrow, tuning his guitar.

"Keep up the good work, Paddy," Sam called, greeting him with a handshake before continuing to the office. He arrived three seconds before 7:30, making his way to meeting room 4.49—the Skybox—which overlooked the entire fourth floor.

A large whiteboard dominated one wall; bold letters scrawled across the top:

CASH OR KEYS

Below it, figures outlined the Arrears Index. A list of names ran down the Late Arrears column.

His team was already seated. Roy Benz, the grizzled veteran of the group, with his dishevelled appearance and perpetual complaints. Sean Hogan, the ex-soldier, is disciplined and meticulous, thriving on order. Mansimar "Mans" Khan is an ambitious young finance grad with an easy charm.

And Mary Swanson, the team's moral compass, a no-nonsense Ethiopian Australian who often challenged Sam's tactics.

Sam leaned against the whiteboard. "The arrears index went up two points overnight," he announced. "That's five days in a row of us going backwards."

Mans groaned. "If the clients actually answered their phones, we wouldn't have this problem."

"That's why they're in Late Arrears," Sean countered. "People who don't pay their bills don't like answering calls."

Roy leaned forward. "We need more skip tracing. Confirm where these debtors live, get a mercantile agent out there, and repossess the cars. Then they'll be calling us."

"They do answer the phone," Mary interjected, "the trouble is we then launch into a demand for payment, or we'll take the car, and in most cases, they don't have the money."

"That's why they need to hand over the car," Sam stated matter-of-factly. "These aren't credit cards; they're secured loans."

Sean nodded. "It's not a choice."

"Exactly," Sam said. "But we can make it work for them. If we let them sell the car privately - and I stress the word agree - they avoid auction and agent fees, which can run into the thousands.

Make them see that." At that moment, the door swung open. Logan Johnstone, a well-groomed, amiable young man in his early twenties dressed in a suit and popular amongst the Late Arrears group, pokes his nose in.

"Hey guys," Logan greeted cheerily.

"Ah, wrong meeting, Logan" Roy reacted, "your team is in the small room, reflective of the team's performance."

"Griggsy is running late" Logan responded, "and not according to the latest figures - our team is on top."

"Which is where we will stay," booms Ian Griggs, a bearded, portly fellow in his early thirties, emerging from behind Logan, who grins before giving a courteous wave as he heads on his merry way to his desk. Griggsy, however, stays.

"Trying to learn a few of our trade secrets, Griggsy," Sam quips, unsure why Griggsy didn't follow Logan.

"Just admiring the scenery, Sam," Griggsy replied as he eyed up Sam's team before bidding farewell. "Have a good day, people," as he heads out the door.

Sam refocused. "We need to get the index down. Treasury's getting nervous. If we don't pull it back by month's end, our borrowing rates might go up."

Roy sensed an opportunity: "Then we shorten the grace period before engaging agents. One week instead of three."

Mary's eyes flared. "What, one week of working an account, and if we don't make contact, we engage mercantile agents?" Mary cried. "That is nor fair on our customers. As I always say, if they are doing it hard financially, they will be doing it hard mentally."

"And the best way to alleviate that mental strife," Sam interjected, "is to sell the car. Get rid of the vehicle, get rid of the stress. I like your idea, Roy. One week. That's the new rule."

"Don't we need Risk and Control to sign off on this?" Mary asked.

Sam smirked. "We are Risk and Control."

The team stood, heading for the door. Sam pointed to the whiteboard as a final reminder.

"And remember, team—cash or keys, cash or keys."

Chapter 2 It's A Club

Sam followed his team from the Skybox, towards the Late Arrears area, and spotted Gavin "Bulldog" Moore, Stuart O'Beigh and Eric Craven in another meeting room, number 4.33, situated directly opposite the Skybox. Gavin waved Sam over who duly obliges.

"Top of the morning" Sam greeted as he entered the room.

"The only thing at the top is the arrears index" Stuart quipped as Sam joined them seated at the table.

Stuart O'Beigh, Default Management Senior Manager, oversaw Collections, repossessions and under-performing loans which are deemed to be uneconomical and are sold to debt-purchasing companies, usually for 10 cents in the dollar, a lifeline for the bank's balance sheet.

Gavin's right-hand man, Stuart was known as "True-Blue Stu" for his thick Australian accent and unwavering loyalty. At his recent 50th birthday, his career milestone was a badge of honour: 25 years in Collections. His philosophy? A good manager is like a chameleon—your opinion depends on the situation.

Gavin was just as pragmatic, though far more ruthless. His nickname, "Bulldog," came from his relentless pursuit of overdue loans. To him, clients were debtors, and debtors paid. His obsession?

The arrears index—particularly the "61 plus" category, the bank's key performance metric. For two years, Global Car Loans had held the lowest arrears in Australia, and Gavin intended to keep it that way.

"What's your take on the index Sam?" Gavin, a short, stocky fellow in his early 40s with neatly cropped hair and immaculately dressed in an Armani navy blue asked.

"It's stubbornly sitting at 0.5," Sam replied.

"Which is still the best in Australia," Stuart added. "Only half a percent of our loans at sixty-

plus days overdue? Impressive compared to the other banks."

"Yes but we can get it lower," Sam stressed.

A knock at the door interrupted them. Renita Bray, Head of Global Credit, stepped inside. In her mid-fifties, she was lean and athletic, years of marathon training evident in her sharp posture.

"Good morning team, how are we?" Renita asks

They all give the standard "good thanks" response though Sam goes a step further.

"You are looking resplendent today Renita; a fetching outfit and I love the way you have done your hair, while you are looking even fitter than ever, is there an event coming up?' Sam flatteringly posed.

"Thank you Sam" Renita beamed, "I knew you would notice and, yes, the Sydney half marathon is on in 3 weeks."

Gavin cleared his throat. "It's not often we see you here in the Manly office Renita, what's the occasion?"

"I have a few meetings here today Gavin," Renita replied.

"Well it's good timing as we were all just talking about the arrears index which we know is a bit high but we have strategies to get it down." Gavin said confidently.

"Good" Renita responded, "and as I mentioned to you last month, we also need to lower our complaints. They have skyrocketed over the last year, especially our vulnerable clients, and this month is no different, I gather everyone here is aware of it?"

"Of course Renita" Gavin responds assertively, as Sam, Stuart and Eric signal acknowledgement.

"I'm setting up a meeting with you Gavin later today," Renita added "a follow-up to last month." "Sounds good," Gavin warily replied.

"Well have a good day everyone" Renita expressed as she left the room, where the mood had now significantly changed.

"What is that all about Bulldog?" a bemused Eric queried.

Eric, like Stuart, is an unremarkable individual, in his mid 30s and keen to climb the corporate ladder. His other similarities to Stuart are his compliance and sizeable girth.

"I thought this would happen sooner" Gavin responded. "The issue of complaints has been brewing for a while. Renita raised it with me last month, decrying the rising AFCA charges and the high number of 'vulnerable' clients, all scumbags as far as I'm concerned, making a complaint. She reckons it makes the bank look bad, even though Collections is Australia's jewel in the Global crown."

"That's because all the onus falls on us" Sam reacted, "the customer has no accountability, they don't want to pay so they complain. The squeaky wheel gets the oil. Consumer protectionism gone mad."

"It's also because our Complaints team is inept" Stuart interjected, "all complaints lodged to the Australian Financial Complaints Authority must come to us first. We are given the opportunity to resolve the grievance before AFCA gets involved. If our Complaints team could resolve them in the first place, AFCA would stay out of it."

"Resolving complaints more quickly would also help to reduce the index' Sam said. "We have at least ten cars out for repossession that the debtor involved has lodged a complaint meaning we can't touch them until it's sorted. It riles me."

"Yeah well there's not much we can do about them" Gavin said, "but what we can do is up the ante when it comes to repossessions, one of your specialties Sam. I see yet again your team had easily the highest number of repossessions last month. Great work, you are a credit to Collections."

"You can count on me Bulldog" Sam said as he prepared to leave. "Though it's getting harder with all these consumer loans now on the books. Commercial used to be 80% of the book, now it's 50/50."

"What are you seeing Sam?" Gavin asked.

"Debtors are wising up Bulldog" Sam responded. They are parking their cars inside their property meaning we need a court order to repossess. Of course commercial loans don't come under the National Consumer Credit Protection act so we can repossess those. Trouble is we are seeing fewer of them. You need to have a word to the silver fox and tell him we need more applications with an ABN."

"I'm catching up with Mark later today" Gavin said, "I'll have a friendly word."

"See you later at The Staines?" Sam says from the door as he is about to leave.

"Absolutely" Gavin replied, "the club, should always meet, at the pub."

Over at the West Wing of Level 4The clock ticked 8:00 a.m., signalling the opening of the Collections telephone lines. The Late Arrears team was already in full swing.

"Three calls in queue, guys," Logan Johnstone called from his desk beneath a sign reading Late Arrears. Around him, ten employees tackled the growing list of overdue loans.

"Can't complain about them not answering when we ring, if we fail to take a call when they ring us" Logan added.

Late Arrears is made up of 2 teams of 6 people in each within the Car Loans department of Global, a burgeoning financial institution which began 7 years earlier in an office in Melbourne to now having presence in 12 countries, including offices in 4 states across Australia. While the two teams like to compete against each other, their primary focus is to reduce the overdue loans, and they don't care how it's done, whether by clients making payments or cars getting repossessed.

"I have to finish this agent repossession report" Roy cried.

"That can wait Roy" Sam chimed in, returning from his meeting with Gavin et al. "Inbound calls are more important, you know that."

"I know Sam but it's a Porsche and the debtor drives it to a cafe every Tuesday where he stays for about an hour. I want the agents to pounce when he's inside sipping on his cafe latte," as Roy takes one of the three awaiting calls.

"I've got one," said Logan, as his team leader, Ian Griggs, was trawling through his phone, showing no interest in the unfolding event.

The third call was taken but Sam couldn't immediately see by whom as, unlike Roy and Logan, nobody vocally claimed it. Sam quickly browsed the phone lines to find the call was taken by Mary which brought a smile to his face, abandoned call rate saved by the most humble and compassionate member of Late Arrears. Sam looked over and saw her bright mien in full view as she eagerly endeavoured to help a struggling client.

Mary is now into her second year in the Car Loans Collections division. Her sole reason for applying for the position was to get her foot in the door of Global with her ultimate goal to work in the multicultural and

Diversity, Equity and Inclusion areas. A lady of purpose, Mary undertook a degree in Human Resources believing this would help her most in realising her ambitions which included working towards a more egalitarian society. As soon as she completed her degree her eyes were on working for a finance company and she had heard good reports about Global's treatment of its employees.

Born in Ethiopia, Mary arrived in Australia when she was three. That was twenty-five years ago when, in the middle of the Eritrean- Ethiopian war, her parents made the bold decision to flee their war-torn home to settle in Australia. While Mary has no recollection of the harrowing events in her place of birth, she is well versed in what occurred thanks to her father who made a point of recounting various episodes and aspects of the war, stressing the importance of learning about her homeland and understanding the devastation conflict and wars can bring.

"Great effort guys," Sam whooped, contrary to Roy who has ended his call.

"As soon as I told him he had rung Global he hung up the phone. All that mad rushing for nothing." Roy complained.

"It'll be in response to our early morning SMS run, the one where we ask them to ring us but don't put who it's from" Sean clarified.

"They won't answer their phone when we ring them" Roy bemoaned, "and when they do ring us they hang up. That alone should be a reason to repossess the car."

"They don't all hang up Roy" Sam reasoned, "the hang-ups are in the minority."

"It's also a skill to keep them on the phone" Griggsy interjected, before returning to looking at his mobile phone.

Sam notices Mary looking distressed when conversing with the customer. He wanders over to offer her assistance and she places the call on hold.

"Very sad this one Sam," Mary lamented, "the customer passed away and I'm speaking to his wife."

"So where is the car?" Sam immediately asked, seemingly indifferent to the emotional state of the caller.

"I didn't ask Sam" Mary replied defiantly, "I've spent most of the time listening to her cry."

"Yeah well I know it's unfortunate but our primary responsibility is to recover the asset" Sam stressed, "unless the wife is going to pay the loan out in full."

"I don't know," Mary replied.

"So before you put her through to Deceased Estates" Sam pressed, "find out where the car is garaged so we can send an agent out to repossess. I haven't had much to do with these ones when the debtor dies but those I have, took ages to finalise."

Back at room 4.33, Gavin, Stuart and Eric are discussing the looming meeting with Renita "So I've already given Griggsy the heads up that he might be looking after both Late Arrears teams initially" Gavin explained.

"If Renita does want this new vulnerable team" Eric asked, "why not keep Sam in Late Arrears and Griggsy to be that team's leader."

"Because Sam is one of us," Gavin replied, "a member of the club. He thinks like me and does whatever I ask of him, complete trust. Griggsy may well come on board, and is showing good signs, but he's not there yet."

"We don't want someone who might go soft on the debtors" Stuart added, "and buy into their bullshit sob stories."

"Sam is the man," Gavin concluded confidently.

At The Corso Sam has taken a break to have a chat with his good mate Paddy Roach who is sitting on his own in the Buskers Burrow, acoustic guitar in hand and playing "Cavatina".

"That's not a bad piece Paddy" Sam said, "I've heard it before but can't nail the title."

"Cavatina" Paddy replied, "written by Stanley Myers." Sam pulled out his phone and looked him up on Google.

"Oh yeah," Sam said, "wrote a lot of music scores. Died in 1993? How do you know about him?"

"Christopher Walken" Paddy replied, "whom I met."

"You've met Christopher Walken?" Sam asked, "that guy is a legend. He was unreal in Pulp.

Fiction. When did you meet him?"

"Um" Paddy said, "gee whiz, let's see, about twenty-three years ago."

"Twenty-three years ago Paddy, you were two," Sam reacted aporetically.

"I know" Paddy said, "there was a movie being made in Cairns and Christopher Walken was in it. My dad went to pick up Mum from work and when he parked the car he was told by somebody there was a movie scene being shot at the nearby beach. So Dad wandered over, carrying me in his arms at the time, and saw Christopher Walken and bowled on up to him and started chatting. Walken looked at me, apparently, and Dad informed him that I'd just turned two years old.

And you know what Christopher Walken said: 'yeah, wish I were two." Paddy said imitating the actor. "Years ago when my dad recounted the story to me, for about the ninth time, he mentioned that Christopher Walken was in his favourite movie - The Deer Hunter, which also featured Robert De Niro. And the theme song to the Deer Hunter was .... Cavatina."

Paddy plays more freely and even though he was not officially performing, he plays it so well a crowd begins to form.

https://www.youtube.com/watch?v=xAAiYMgFcbw

Chapter 3 Abbey

In a two-bedroom unit in the leafy northern Sydney suburb of Turramurra, Abbey Jones prepared for another day at work. Her routine included dropping off her five-year-old son, Vincent, at primary school before heading into the city.

Abbey and Sam had met at Wollongong University in their first year—she was studying Psychology, he was studying Journalism. It was Abbey's striking smile, slender figure, and long blonde hair that first caught Sam's attention, but it was her kindness, trust, and caring nature that kept him. Two months into their relationship, Sam had surprised her with a weekend getaway to the Gold Coast. Four months later, they moved in together.

But eighteen months into the relationship something unplanned and unforeseen happened:

Abbey became pregnant. Sam was adamant Abbey should have an abortion, reasoning there was plenty of time to have children later, when they were settled and graduated from university. And at twenty three years of age he was in no mood or mental capacity to become a father. Abbey was equally adamant they should keep the life growing inside of her and six months after they learned of her pregnancy, her wishes were realised.

After dropping Vincent off at 8.15, Abbey drove to the Turramurra train station, parked her car in the all-day free section, and caught the next train into the city.

Abbey alighted at the Wynyard station and headed to the office in Barangaroo, nestled in Sydney's central business district, where she works as the executive assistant for IVF fertility specialist, Mark Levene. Though today is Tuesday it is Abbey's first working day of the week, thanks to the generosity afforded by Mark in furnishing a flexible four-day working week while paying her for five, enabling Abbey to continue her studies, albeit now part-time as opposed to initially being full-time.

Logging into her computer, she found that Alex, Mark's partner, had — true to form — already contacted all the upcoming clients, streamlining Abbey's workload to a few confirmation texts.

She pressed play on the voicemail and listened to four messages as Mark breezed into the office, his usual beaming smile in place.

"Good morning" Mark, "how are you Abbey, how was uni and how are we looking?"

"Good morning Mark," Abbey replied, "good, pretty good and very good, Alex has, as usual, organised everything superbly. Your first consultation is with Rita Dyer. She and her partner have been married for five years, no children. As for uni, I had to leave early, missing an important lecture in the process as I had to pick up Vincent from school and afterwards we both went to a movie."

Abbey is half-way into a 4-year psychology degree, a course which began seven years earlier but went from full-time to part-time to enable her to care for Vincent. Contrary to Sam who didn't need to delay a day, completing his degree in the three scheduled years.

"I thought that his nibs was supposed to pick up Vincent" Mark asked.

"Sam found another reason not to" Abbey responded, "I couldn't be bothered arguing with him this time."

"You know" Mark said, "now that Alex has such a good handle on things, I was thinking we could change you to a three-day week to help you finish your degree sooner."

Abbey looked directly at Mark, digesting his proposal. She never wanted to go part-time in the first place but Sam's selfish departure, not the birth of Vincent, forced her hand. Her mind wandered back to the moment Sam packed his bags where she yelled at him as he headed out the door, "I'm not going to let this stop me from completing my degree."

"Food for thought Abbey" Mark added as he headed towards his office.

Across the City

At the outdoor setting of The Staines Hotel, a popular local tavern situated directly opposite the

Manly beach, Gavin, Stuart and Eric discuss the latest month's results for Car Loans Collections while downing a swag of schooners. Stuart is about to head to the bar when they are joined by Sam.

"Sorry I'm late fellas" Sam apologised, "I thought this was booked for the Skybox. We don't normally meet this early here."

"Couldn't get a room, all booked out" Stuart explained. "Carlton draught?"

"Oooh" Sam reacted, "maybe not Stuart. I love a beer but 9.30 in the morning is a bit too early"

"Too early?" Gavin interjected as he held up his three/quarter empty glass, indicating to Stuart he'd like another, "drinking makes other people more interesting" bringing a chortle from Eric.

"Besides, this is the best meeting room of all, it's where we have our most productive and ideas-driven gatherings."

"Especially when you have an ad hoc meeting with the director later on" Eric quipped.

"Still haven't had it?" Sam asked.

"In about thirty-three minutes," Gavin replied. "No agenda, but we all know what it's about.

Renita's worried about the complaints. But complaints come with the territory in Collections. Nothing new. And I wouldn't call this meeting ad hoc, plenty of planning going on here" as he polishes off the remainder of his schooner.

Stuart returns empty handed. "They're out of Carlton as they are having to replace the keg but they have it in mid-strength" he reveals.

"Mid-strength" Gavin reacts dismissively, "having a mid-strength would be like going to a brothel and getting a hug. Just give me a Stone and Wood."

Sam has not been fully informed by Gavin of the likely contents of the meeting, believing it is likely to revolve around lofty complaint levels and the arrears index.

"As I'm sure there has been with Renita" Sam observed. "You may want to remind her that while the complaints and arrears may be up, our dollars collected is also at an all-time high, we are getting more debtors to pay. It's not our fault the Sales team write so many lousy loans."

"Don't let the silver fox hear you say that Sam" Eric remarked, "though it sure has been a good month, it was a godsend getting the proceeds from the SUV auction right on the last day."

"And how good was that repossession from the Day Care centre?" Stuart interjected, returning clasping three schooners.

"Yeah" Sam responded with a grin. "That was poetry in motion."

"Scholes were exceptional there" Gavin added, "the mum kept parking the car in her garage so, as we know, being a consumer loan, we couldn't repossess unless it's parked outside her property. She was too cunning for that and never left it on the side of the road, always in her driveway, as if to taunt us. So they waited until she dropped her kids off at daycare and when she was inside they swooped. I agree boys, one of the highlights of a great month."

"The highlight," Sam added. "And the agents did the right thing by the mum by allowing her time to remove the baby seat and toys from the back seat before they towed the car. You'll kill it with Renita Bulldog, you will tell her the real story."

"Well, gotta go" Gavin uttered, as he skulls the schooner just provided by Stuart, "can't keep Ren waiting."

Sam glanced at his watch and decided to shorten his stay.

"I'll head back too guys" Sam added, "I need to ensure the team is at full throttle, but I'll see you back here in a few hours."

Back at the Office

After darting back across the road, Sam took the lift to level 4 and headed towards his team.

Along the way he notices a former colleague, Ali Hasan who has just finished a call. Ali, a gentle and amiable fellow in his mid-50s previously worked in Collections but moved to a less confronting role in the Hardship team, preferring to help clients who are unable to pay rather than applying the blowtorch to people who are struggling.

"Ali, me ol' mate, how is life treating you?" Sam beams as they shake hands.

"Pretty good Sam, though that call was tough," Ali replied. "A twenty-three-year-old lady ringing from a mental facility."

"What did you do?" Sam enquired.

"Three months no payments" Ali responded.

Sam peered at the account on Ali's screen.

"A Mustang" Sam blurted, "why does she need a Ford Mustang?"

Brianna V'Landys, a petite lady in her late twenties with dark, shoulder-length hair and Hardship's and Ali's team leader, appeared out of nowhere and joins the discussion.

"Stopping my team from working again Sam?" Brianna interjects with a wry grin.

"Hello Bree" Sam responded, "just learning about the Hardship caper as well as admiring the scenery, especially the way you have done your hair, makes you glow even more."

"Flattery will get you everywhere Sam" Brianna asserted "but I am sure you have plenty to do in Late Arrears."

"We sing from the same hymn book Bree" Sam quipped, "I am about to head off on my merry way, good seeing you both."

As Sam leaves he turns to Ali: "three months no payments" he says with a slight shake of the head, "Should've just taken back the car, it would be a win win."

Back in Late Arrears

Sam found his team in celebratory mode - Scholes have repossessed a Mercedes AMG. Roy is particularly chuffed.

Global engages Scholes Mercantile to execute three functions, all concerning overdue loans, and designed to be in this order. Firstly, a field call where Global's attempts to contact a client have been fruitless so a Scholes agent is directed to speak to the client to discuss the situation. Secondly, instructions for the mercantile agent to seek payment for the arrears and finally, if the first two are unsuccessful, repossession. The Late Arrears team, though, often ignore the first two and dive straight to function number three.

"I told you skip tracing is the key to finding these recalcitrant debtors" Roy boomed at Sam as Sean shook his hand, congratulating him on another win for the team.

"OK" Sam prompted, "what am I missing?"

"The merc, AMG" Logan interjected, "Scholes collected it today."

"A hundred and forty grand" Sam mused, "that will make a dent in the index."

"I thought you had meetings at your favourite venue Sam" Mary interjected.

"I did" Sam responded, "and I still do but something told me I needed to be back here, with all the action. How can you not love Collections" he beamed.

In Room 4.33

Renita was leading the meeting with Gavin who sat silently and dispassionately digesting her words.

"Everything has already been formulated for the design and execution of this new team, you just need to ensure it operates efficiently and as directed." Renita explained.

"So the manager of this new team will report to me?" Gavin asked.

"That's right Gavin" Renita answered, "you will also get to decide who is in the team, who leads it, I thought maybe lan Griggs would be suitable but it will be your call. Critically though, we will need to see: A, a significant drop in complaints stemming from Collections, and B, greater care for our vulnerable clients. It's a big opportunity for everyone involved Gavin."

Outside on The Manly Corso

About one hundred metres from The Staines and a similar distance from the beach, Paddy

Roach is enjoying a break, sipping on a cup of English breakfast tea as he sits next to a keyboard in The Burrow.

Paddy, a solidly built fellow tipping the scales at 94 kilograms and standing just over 6 feet tall, has made Manly his home for the last two years since piling his Holden Commodore with his prized possessions: an acoustic guitar, keyboard, harmonica and didgeridoo after impulsively deciding to leave his birthplace of Cairns where he lived for the first twenty years of his life with his parents and three siblings.

That was five years ago and his travels took him to almost every town and city of Australia, performing as a busker to pay his way. A talented musician, he attracted a sizeable audience wherever he played, leading to a relatively prosperous lifestyle but after three years he began to tire of his nomadic existence and considered the pros and cons of settling down. And when he drove into Manly, his mind was made up, here they were all pros.

It wasn't just the spectacular surf beach, the friendly locals, bush trails or sweeping harbour views which grabbed him, Paddy was especially taken by the hive of activity in The Manly Corso.

Essentially a pedestrian strip with a wide variety of shops and pubs on either side, The Corso gave Paddy an adrenaline rush with its oozing of energy and positive people. He also liked that The Corso contained street performers which gave him the idea of creating an area assigned solely for buskers, where he could ply his trade and, hopefully, attract other musicians to join him. After approaching the Manly council and performing to the Mayor and her councillors, he convinced them to set aside a designated area in The Corso for buskers to perform. Apart from committing to keeping the area clean and seemly, Paddy wanted to make The Burrow a place where any aspiring musician could play and soon there was a lengthy list of buskers knocking on his door expressing a keenness to play. As a result, Paddy created a schedule and list of regular artists and while he would sometimes perform solo, he regularly played his vast array of instruments in a supporting capacity for his fellow buskers.

As he finishes his tea, Paddy sees Sam, talking on his phone, walking towards him. Sam met Paddy about two years ago and their mutual love of playing music has helped them in becoming very close friends. Sam keeps his personal life away from his work colleagues but there is little about him that Paddy doesn't know, and vice-versa.

"I just can't do it Abbey" Sam said as he sat down next to Paddy, "sorry but I have to go" as he ended the call.

"The missus?" Paddy asked.

"Ex-missus Paddy" Sam replied, "you know that. She wanted me to look after Vince but I can't."

"Why not?" Paddy asked, "what out of the ordinary do you have on?"

"Well, nothing," Sam reacted, "but I have a lot on, you know what I mean."

As quick as look at you, Paddy rises from the Burrow step to sit on the chair behind his keyboard. He then begins playing and is joined by a young, slender fellow wearing large glasses and long, unkempt dark hair. He is also carrying a trumpet which he begins to play after 20 seconds of Paddy's introduction to Herb Alpert's "Rise".

https://www.youtube.com/watch?v=vltC-O7PDYQ

Chapter 4 Sensitive Matters

At 7.27 a.m. Sam is at his desk, reviewing loan contracts which are in the hands of mercantile agents when he receives an invitation from Gavin to attend a meeting at 7.30 in room number 4.38, one of the seven designated areas for formal gatherings on the fourth floor.

As he made his way through the office, Sam spotted Johnny Kep at his desk, a solitary figure buried in his computer screen. True to form, Sam made a slight detour to say hello.

Johnny Kepler, better known as Johnny Kep, was a wiry, greying-haired man in his late 30s, standing just under six feet tall. With 18 years of experience in repossessions, he was a walking encyclopaedia on the subject. Despite his wealth of knowledge, Johnny preferred to keep to himself, though he appreciated the interest Sam showed in his passion—photography.

"These are from Dorrigo National Park, in Coffs Harbour" Johnny says proudly, "had the perfect weather for it too."

"You drove all the way to Coffs Harbour for this" Sam asked, "must've been what, a five hour trip?"

"Six" Johnny replied, "but it was well worth it, that park is sublime."

"What makes that place more special than the national parks in Sydney?" Sam asked

"Nothing Sam" Johnny replied, "they're also wonderful, I go to those too. We have more great national parks than you could poke a stick at."

"Well they look amazing Johnny" Sam said, "I can imagine you had a whale of a time in Coffs.

I've got a meeting with Bulldog so I'll catch you later."

The Meeting

Thirty seconds later, Sam entered Room 4.38 where Gavin sat at the head of the table, flanked by Stuart and Eric.

"Hey Bulldog" Sam greeted, "I gather this sudden catch-up is on the back of the meeting you had with Renita."

"It certainly is Sam" Gavin responded, "it certainly is."

"Sounds ominous," Sam retorted.

"Not at all Sam" Gavin replied, "it's good news, especially for you."

Sam raised an eyebrow as his gaze landed on the large whiteboard behind Gavin, where bold lettering listed:

SENSITIVE MATTERS

1. Mental health or mental capacity limitations

1. Domestic and Family Violence

2. Homelessness or temporary accommodation

3. Financial Abuse

4. Elder Abuse

5. Terminal illness and/or long-term illness

6. Natural disasters

7. Deceased Estates

8. Threats of self-harm or harm to others

NOT A SENSITIVE MATTER

1. Incarceration

2. Workers' Compensation

3. Maternity Leave

4. Anxiety

5. Emergency Expense

6. Divorce/separation

7. Unemployment

8. Over committed

9. Bankruptcy

10. Bludging

"As you know" Gavin continued "we've been receiving a few complaints about our aggressive, yet fair and principled, approach to collecting overdue payments. Some have ended up with the ombudsman which is not only bad for our reputation but it's also very costly. We all know it's a silly system where financial institutions pay for the costs of a customer complaint, often getting into the thousands of dollars but it is what it is."

"That's because these debtors know how to play the system" Sam interjected, "you know that Bulldog, consumer protectionism gone mad."

Gavin nodded while Eric continued to type away on his laptop. Stuart had his ears to the conversation with one eye on Sam and the other on the whiteboard, double-checking what he had written was correct.

"Renita believes our processes are inconsistent and too reliant on individual discretion" Gavin continued, "I don't necessarily agree but we do think it's a good idea to create a team specifically for these cases. And we want you to run it."

"Complaints?" a perplexed Sam questioned, "you want me to manage complaints?"

"No, no" Gavin clarified, "we already have a team for that."

"A team," Stuart interjected, "which does a lousy job."

"Your new team," Gavin advised, "will still be collections - after all you are the best - but it will be collections for our most vulnerable clients."

"Sensitive collections" Stuart added.

"Hence the whiteboard" Sam remarked as he peered past Gavin's shoulder, indicating what stood behind him.

"That's right," Stuart added, "you will manage a team of four where your portfolio will consist of what we describe as, as Bulldog said, our vulnerable clients. Customers who are affected by domestic violence, mental illness, financial abuse, deceased estates, loss of family members etc. It's all on the whiteboard."

"I value your knowledge and guidance Bulldog, you know that" Sam responds, "but this sounds like a bad idea. Debtors already get away with blue murder and this will only give them more reasons to avoid paying. But also, I barely have a sensitive bone in my body, I love getting debtors to pay when they are behind on payments and squeal for mercy."

"I hear you Sam," Bulldog reacted, "but this is not what you are thinking. See this as an opportunity."

"So does this mean we won't be able to repossess cars?" a slightly dejected Sam asked.

"Of course not," Gavin fired back, "you will still get to do what you love most, repossessions will be a critical part of the team, we just want you to be a bit nicer to the debtor when you do it. With your vocabulary and use of words, we feel you will be ideal for what will be a challenging but rewarding role."

"And one you can easily handle," Stuart said encouragingly.

"You're also getting a promotion Sam" Eric chimed in, "to manager."

Sam's demeanour was starting to ease. He'd always wanted to become a manager and beyond and started to see the potential in the new role.

"It will also display your versatility Sam" Bulldog added, "when you master this position it will speak volumes on your resume."

"OK" Sam acknowledged, "sounds promising. So I'm still reporting to Eric?" as he looks over at his current boss.

"You'll be reporting directly to me," Gavin replied.

"That's one of the reasons I am here Sam" Eric explained, "treat this as a handover - and congratulations."

"Thanks Eric," Sam replied, "you've been good to me."

"What," Gavin said with a wry smile, "are you implying I won't be?"

"Of course not Bulldog" Sam said, "just giving credit where credit is due as Eric reaches out to shake Sam's hand.

The New Team

"So you will still undertake collections and endeavour to bring accounts up-to-date but you will be afforded more leniency when dealing with those more challenging sensitive matters." Gavin elaborated.

"What kind of leniency?" Sam asked.

"All of these contracts will be coded to "Vulnerable" and will be kept away from the general collections processes" Stuart explained.

"NODS?" Sam posed.

"You will still need to issue notices of demand" Gavin replied, "we legally cannot repossess without doing it. A big part of your role will be to convince non-paying debtors to return the asset willingly, a voluntary surrender but a genuine voluntary surrender. Repossessions bring in too many complaints for Renita's liking so we need to sway them to think they are doing it of their own volition.

Make them think it's like one of those plea deals the courts embark on. You know how their selling point is that the defendant doesn't have to go through the ordeal of a trial. They might be innocent but it allows them to move on with their life. It's no different here."

"I think what you are referring to there Bulldog is the Alford Plea" Sam observed.

"Whatever" Gavin said, "It's a way of making them think they are picking the best worst case scenario. You will still engage mercantile agents etc" Bulldog added, "and I want to get a weekly update and once a month you are to produce a report which the senior leadership team will read."

"Wow" a chuffed Sam expressed, "this means my delegations levels change, Level 4-"

"You will still need to run everything by me first Sam" Gavin stressed, "we are part of a club and everything you think of doing needs my approval. You know the drill, anything that happens is shared with us first, I don't get to hear of something new from someone else first."

"Can't have you going rogue," Stuart laughed.

Sam looked at the whiteboard and accepted everything looked clear-cut, except one.

"Looks straightforward guys" Sam acknowledged, "though I thought anxiety was classified as a mental illness, shouldn't that be a reason to code to Sensitive Matters?"

"It was suggested but I wanted it removed" Bulldog replied, "anxiety is a good thing. Being anxious means you care. And if you're not anxious you become complacent and payments are not made."

"Of course fellas" Sam stressed, "I was only kidding. And a team of four?" Where are they going to come from? Do I get a say in who they are?"

"The four includes you Sam" Gavin clarified, "so you will have three direct reports, and no, you don't have a say but I am sure you will like who they are. Logan, Brianna and Mary."

"Brianna?" a surprised Sam asked, "Hardship team leader Brianna?"

"That's her," Gavin replied.

"Gee whiz Bulldog" Sam pondered, "I don't know that she will like the idea of reporting to me."

"Everyone likes reporting to you Sam" Stuart quipped.

"Brianna has a lot of knowledge and experience with hardship/vulnerable customers," Gavin added, "she will be a big help for you."

"Logan and Mary though," Sam beamed as he warmed to the new role, "inspired choices."

"I especially like Logan" Bulldog remarked, "I think he will be a good fit. He is a pretty cultured and refined fellow."

"He is?" Sam reacted, "I wasn't aware but that is good to know" Sam knew Logan fairly well and hadn't seen any evidence of "refinement" or "cultured". While Logan liked to dress in a suit, they were the cheapest available and he only did it to cover his tattoos.

Sam then thought about what will be left behind.

"I will miss my current team though, "Sam added, "who's going to be their TL now?"

"Griggsy," Eric replied.

Gavin leaned in. "This fits in perfectly with your ambitions Sam. Do well and assistant director is next."

"We will also need to design a policy Bulldog" Stuart interrupted.

"It is also worth pointing out Sam" Gavin remarked, "that Renita initially wanted Griggsy for the role but I made a strong case for you and she agreed."

"Really?" Sam responded, unsure at this point whether the move would be beneficial or not, "I am sure Griggsy would've been all right."

"Yeah but he's not part of the club," Gavin asserted.

"Not yet," Stuart uttered.

"You and I think alike Sam" Bulldog added, "we are two peas in a pod. That's why you are part of the club."

At that moment, Raj Singh, head of Workflow, the team which orchestrates the contracts and schedules for the LA team to work each day, walked in the door.

"Hey Raj" Sam greeted, "what's cooking?"

"Thanks for jumping onto this at late notice Raj" Gavin acknowledged.

"No probs Bulldog," Raj reacted, "anything for the club."

"Congrats on the new role mate" Raj says to Sam, "a big task but you are the right man for the job."

"Thanks pal" Sam said, "I imagine you are here to give me the rundown."

"I've booked a room for 11 o'clock so I can take you through the new workflow" Raj replied.

"I checked your calendar which indicates you are free then."

"Sure Raj" Sam acknowledges, aware Gavin wants to consult with Raj to ensure the workflow meets his requirements, as he rises from his chair and heads to the door.

"And what will the name of this new department be?" Sam asked Gavin, Stuart, and Eric answered in unison: "Sensitive Matters"

Dorrigo National Park

Chapter 5 The Preparation

Monday morning dawned, and as the clock ticked past 7 a.m., Sam was already at his desk, preparing for his first team meeting under the Sensitive Matters banner. He had arrived earlier than usual, eager to set the right tone for his new role.

As he reviewed the performance reports of his new team members, a familiar voice broke his concentration.

"Good morning, Sam. You're here even earlier than usual," Angie, one of Global's cleaners, chirped cheerfully as she pushed a trolley stacked with food supplies towards the kitchen.

"And a very good morning to you, Angie. You're looking as spiffing as ever," Sam replied, flashing his signature grin. "And yes, today a new opportunity dawns."

Angie grabbed a banana, a peach, and an apple from her tray and placed them on Sam's desk.

"As does every day," she replied with a smile before continuing on her way.

Sam skimmed through the performance reports, impressed with Logan's but taken aback by Brianna's.

Despite holding the highest employee level in the team, her review painted a picture of a struggling leader— complaints from direct reports, concerns from HR, and a final recommendation to reassess her role.

Logan's report, in contrast, highlighted his popularity among colleagues but also his lack of career direction. Four roles in two years suggested someone unsure of his path. Even his self-submitted career goals read simply: TBA.

Mary's review, however, was exactly what Sam expected. Passionate about people, her long-term goal was to join Global's Diversity, Equity and Inclusion team in New York. She had already founded the division's D&I group, despite Gavin's initial resistance. Sam smiled—Mary was a perfect fit for Sensitive Matters.

His thoughts were interrupted by an incoming email from Gavin, addressed to Collections, Customer Service, Novated Leasing, Sales, Credit, and Workflow, with Renita and Jason Mooney CC'd.

Effective tomorrow, all clients falling into the following categories will now be managed by our Sensitive

Matters team and should be directed accordingly. The corresponding codes for each category are as follows...

Sam barely had time to digest the details before a heavy bag thudded onto the desk beside him.

"Ian Griggs?" Sam smirked. "Gee whiz, Griggsy, who kicked you out of bed? You haven't been this early since Big Ben was a wristwatch."

"Gotta prepare myself for the big change," Ian remarked.

"Congrats on taking over my team" Sam acknowledged.

"Yes mate," Griggsy replied, "big shoes to fill. And congratulations to you Sam. Sensitive Matters, I can see that becoming a household name."

Sam wasn't sure what Griggsy meant by that. Though they had worked together for two years, Sam was always wary of Griggsy's motives, having come to the conclusion Ian would do anything to get a promotion, even if it were at the expense of his own team members.

"Well you are going to have a lot on your plate now Griggsy, "Sam said, "looking after two teams."

"And Hannah and I have just had our second child so it's all happening in twos" Griggsy quipped.

"It's only temporary though, right" Sam remarked with a hint of a question to subtly seek confirmation the change was short-term.

"Yeah well Bulldog told me the gig is temporary until they find your replacement" Ian responded, "but I want to prove I can look after both and that I am management material."

"Good for you pal" Sam responded, "though you may have to hold your horses on the notion of looking after two teams, I'm not convinced this is the role for me and could be back donning the TL hat as quick as look at you."

"From what I hear Sam" Griggsy reacted, "it's a done deal, there is no going back, all roads point to Sensitive Matters. Besides, you're now a manager."

Sam digested Griggsy's comments before responding, "yeah, you're probably right. It's just a bit hard at the moment getting my head around the whole Sensitive Matters concept and the functions that go with it.

Whatever happens, I am sure my team will flourish under you."

"Former team" Griggsy quipped.

Sam returns to his computer and schedules a meeting with Brianna, Mary and Logan, booking

4.11, the smallest room on the floor but the only one available. He titles the meeting "Sensitive Matters

Debrief" and sends them the invitation.

Needing a break, he headed to the in-house coffee shop for a cappuccino and a jam doughnut.

On his way down the stairs, he spotted Renita heading up.

"Hey Sam" Renita beamed, "congratulations."

"Thanks, Renita," Sam replied casually.

"This is an important role," she emphasised. "A lot of very senior people are watching. We've had a disturbing number of complaints from vulnerable clients. Some of the things I've seen—" she shook her head. "I need you to make sure they're treated well. And frankly, I can't think of anyone better for the job."

"That's very kind of you," Sam acknowledged. "How much longer are you in Manly?"

"Last day today," she replied before heading towards the Skybox.

"Enjoy your day full of meetings," Sam quipped, earning a chuckle from her.

As Sam waited for his cappuccino, his phone rang. It was Abbey, his ex-partner. Sam and Abbey were together for 3 years and have a 5-year-old son, Vincent, the custody of which is shared though not evenly.

"Hi Abbey," Sam answered.

"Hi Sam" Abbey greeted, "how are you?"

"Flat out like a lizard drinking" Sam replied, "what's up?"

"I was wondering" Abbey replied, "if you could look after Vincent this weekend as my mum is not well and I'd like to see her."

"It's not my turn this weekend" Sam reacted, "you know that. My weekend is the one after this one."

"I know," Abbey replied, "and I'm sorry for dropping this on you but I only just learned of it and getting to Queensland will-"

"Look I have to go" Sam interrupted. "It's really busy here. I'm sorry to hear about your mum but you'll just have to take Vincent with you. As we both know, you agreed I would look after Vince every third weekend. I mean what is the point of agreeing to something if you are just going to turn around and renege on it?"

There was a long pause from Abbey and as Sam was about to say something the line dropped out.

Meeting Room 4.11

Brianna and Mary didn't bother logging in at their desk, they both read Sam's meeting invitation on the train on their way into the office so headed directly to meeting room 4.11. It was 8.00 a.m. with the meeting not due to start for another 12 minutes.

"I heard a while ago there were going to be some changes "Brianna remarked, "primarily due to the rise in complaints."

"I only got told on Friday" Mary revealed, "that I was going to this new Sensitive Matters team, but I didn't know who else would be involved, other than Sam of course. I certainly wasn't aware you'd be in the team. So are you-"

"I'm still a level 3," Brianna muttered, "just not a team leader anymore."

Sam walked in. "Greetings ladies, aren't you both a sight for sore eyes."

"Hi Sam" Mary chirps while Brianna stays silent.

"So Brianna and Mary" Sam said "welcome to Sensitive Matters."

"Are we it?" Brianna asked incredulously

"One more" Sam replied, "Logan Johnstone, a team of superstars. Before he arrives, and something I have discovered is Logan has a penchant for arriving at the last minute, how are we feeling about this development?"

"I think it's a good move" Mary replied, "I'm feeling very excited"

"As the old saying goes, Mary" Sam said, "choose a job you love and you'll never work a day in your life," aware that while he has his personal reservations about the new role, he must always be positive and upbeat for his team.

"Well I'm not excited" Brianna conveyed, "it's all very well for you Mary, this is a promotion for you whereas it is a demotion for me."

"It is definitely not a demotion Brianna, "Sam stressed "you still retain your Level 3 status, it is a change of role, not a demotion."

"I've gone from leading a team of eight direct reports" Brianna snapped, "to having nobody and now I report to you. Sounds like a demotion to me."

The door opens and Logan walks in. Sam looks at his watch which reads 8.00.

"Hi guys" Logan greeted, "how are we all?"

"Welcome Logan" Sam responded "the meeting was scheduled for 8.00 - and you arrive at 8.00"

"Well you know what they say" Logan quipped, "leave it to the last minute and it only takes a minute."

"Well welcome to Sensitive Matters Logan" Sam saluted, "we were just discussing how everyone feels about the new team."

Silence descended as Logan looked at Brianna and Mary, expecting one or both to respond.

When they didn't Logan offered his thoughts.

"For me it's hard to say," Logan replied. "I've changed roles in the last two years more times than I've changed my socks so what's another one I guess. I was hoping, after my good yearly reviews I'd be getting a promotion which, and correct me if I am wrong Sam, doesn't seem to be the case."

"Well" Sam responded, "if you base it on the status level it would not be a promotion but on the level of importance to the business it is a promotion."

"So really" Logan sought to clarify, "it is a sideways move?"

"As they say Logan," Sam responded, "sometimes you need to move sideways to move up."

"Well I see this as God looking after me" Mary beamed, "what a great opportunity. A specialist team helping our most vulnerable clients, what a privilege."

"I didn't know you were religious Mary" Sam quizzed.

"I'm not" Mary responded, "I just have great faith in God and how much he looks after me."

"I guess you could call that a GLAM" Sam quipped.

Mary and Brianna looked at each other with puzzled looks on their faces.

"God Looks After Me" Sam explained "a GLAM."

"I gather it's a GLAM for you too Sam?" Brianna noted a little begrudgingly. "Get a promotion did we?"

"Um, yeah," Sam replied. "I'm now a manager, L4"

Sam sensed the meeting had not begun to his liking and tried to change the mood.

"Can we quit with all the talk about promotion and demotion and side-otion, and most especially - emotion" Sam implored. "As Mary said, this is a good thing, a real opportunity to shine.

Once we spend a bit more time digesting the concept and getting your heads around what this is all about, I am sure we will all be singing from the same hymn book."

"Nah you're right" Logan conceded, "sorry to appear ungrateful."

"Good as gold" Sam acknowledged, "I know this is all very sudden and a bit of a shock but I tell you what, we have one heck of a team."

The atmosphere moderates and Brianna manages to eke out a smile.

"We're all in this together team, " Sam said. "Now, let's talk about portfolios..."

Chapter 6 Anyone with A Pulse

It is standing room only in the Skybox with the Car Loans General Manager, Jason Mooney chairing a meeting, attended by all the department heads including Renita, Gavin and Stuart, with the theme and purpose to focus on selling more loans. Eric is there, seated next to Gavin and Mark Bryers, the leading Business Development Manager (BDM) known for his sharp suits, composed mien, smooth delivery and thick thatch of grey hair.

"Are they all here?" Jason posed.

"All but one" Renita quipped

"I'm going anyway," Jason added. There were a few chuckles from some around the table as this was an in-house joke amongst a few of them as Jason liked using movie quotes in his presentations.

Jason, to whom some in the Collections team snidely refer to as "the jockey" due to his slight frame, a fraction over five feet tall and barely tipping the scales at 55 kilograms, was also an avid movie buff and often his daily discourse and lingo, including meetings and formal presentations, contained quotes from his favourite films.

"Glengarry Glen Ross jokes aside" Jason continued, "there are some similarities with what I am about to articulate because, like the movie, it's all about sales and getting them to sign on the line that is dotted. "

Jason walked to the whiteboard at the front of the room and removed the covering blank sheet to unveil a five-point strategy.

1. Current Loan Balance: $5billion

2. Projected Loan Balance - by 30 June - $14billion

3. EBANZA dealerships

4. Direct Sales

5. Brokers

"This is our road map," Jason declared. "Right now our loan book is hovering just below $5billion and 250,000 individual loans, which I think is a fraction of what we are capable of achieving."

"$5billion to $14billion?" Mark interjected, "'that's an increase of almost 200% in 10 Months."

Mark Bryers is often likened by his car loans colleagues to Gavin, primarily because they both dress resplendently, have glistening whitened teeth, innately inveigling and each bearing a thick mane of hair - Mark's is silver while Bulldog is mousy brown. While Mark is overtly known as the silver fox, Bulldog is, unbeknown to him, nicknamed by the late arrears team as Mini Me due to his 5 feet 2 inch stature, compared to Mark who is more than a foot taller.

"At face value it sounds a lot" Jason responded, "and as you can see on the whiteboard, number 3 is Ebanza dealerships. Many of you will be pleased to learn that we are in the process of buying that bank's book which is a tick over $5billion so that takes it to $10billion without lifting a finger"

"But that is still an extra four billion which is almost double our existing book" Mark reasoned.

And Global's interest rates aren't exactly on the low side at present, barely even competitive."

Stuart nods at Gavin who is seated next to him. Gavin was one of the few who was privy to this major development, both the Ebanza dealerships purchase and the objective to reach $14billion in loans, which he shared before the meeting with Stuart.

"I want," Jason espoused, "for you all to go harder, sell, sell, sell to basically anyone with a pulse."

Mark scoffed. "We're already doing that, Jason. The problem is Credit taking forever to assess applications. And when they finally do, they nitpick over tiny details and reject solid deals. It's killing us."

"Great point Mark," Jason acknowledged. "That's changing. We're rolling out a new system.

Right now, the average decision time is three days. That's getting slashed to six hours. In some cases,

brokers will get an answer within the hour."

A murmur rippled through the room. That was a game-changer.

Jason continued, "We've tweaked the algorithms on our express application system. Broker-submitted applications will get priority treatment, and anything declined will be reviewed by a senior credit manager with the aim of approving it."

Mark smirked. "So if someone doesn't fit the criteria, we just... make it fit?"

Jason grinned. "Exactly. We have assembled a crack hot collections team," 'This crew is good' winking at Mark who quickly responded to Jason's movie quote, "Heat. Al Pacino, I got an idea of what it is they're looking at" followed by a hearty chortle.

"Spot on Mark" Jason reacted, "and our collections crew know how to collect when the client can't pay. I want us to believe that every time a car is financed, it can be financed through Global."

"And" Gavin interrupted, who was sitting at the front of the table, next to Stuart and a few feet from Jason, "to address the rise in complaints, we've formed a new team called Sensitive Matters.

This team will handle vulnerable clients—those facing financial hardship, domestic violence, mental illness, you name it. The goal is to treat them with care and professionalism while still getting results."

"We've also added it to Kanban" Eric chirped, "currently in progress and I am confident we will be at the completed stage in the not-too-distant future."

On the East Side of Level 4

Johnny Kep sat by the window, scanning the listings for the upcoming Pymbles auction. Thirty-two repossessed Global vehicles were set to go under the hammer the next day. He double-checked the valuations, ensuring the reserves were set correctly.

Sam approached, grinning. "Johnny Kep. How's the land of repossessions?"

Johnny didn't look up. "Busy, Sam. Just checking the auction listings."

Sam peered over his shoulder. "What exactly are you checking for?"

"Valuations," Johnny replied. "Making sure we're not selling too low. If we do, we'll get hit with complaints from debtors claiming we short-changed them."

"Who does the valuations?" Sam quizzed.

"Usually it will be me" Johnny replied "but most of these were done by Pymbles and while they are generally pretty good; on occasion they get it wrong. To give you an example (shows Sam his screen) this Pajero was valued by Pymbles at $11,000 with a reserve of the same but its correct valuation is $16k while I will put a reserve of $18k."

"Why would you put a reserve higher than the valuation?" Sam asked.

"Because I think we can get more," Johnny replied. "This type of car sells well and invariably gets more than for what it is initially valued."

Sam nodded, "like that old golf metaphor - always push for better. A par is fine, but you want a birdie. Then an eagle. Then an albatross. And, if you're lucky, a hole-in-one."

Johnny chuckled. "As long as it's not a double bogey."

"Anyway" Sam said "I need to learn more about the whole repossession process. I feel it will be important now that I am in charge of the vulnerable clients."

"Oh yeah" Johnny exclaimed, "I just saw Bulldog's e-mail, what is that all about?"

They are interrupted by a song which appears to be coming from Johnny's desk. It is "Sympathy For The Devil" by the Rolling Stones and is the ringtone on Johnny's phone. "Sorry Sam" as he answers the call.

"Not at all Johnny" Sam reacted, "your ringtone has reminded me to do something I have wanted for an aeon."

"Hey Ben" Johnny answers on his phone "thanks for ringing back and perfect timing, I need to change a few valuations ……..."

Sam pulls out his phone and endeavours to change his standard ringtone to that of the Everton song, the same one he has on his alarm. As he finishes, so too does Johnny's phone call.

"That was quick," Sam observed.

"Time is of the essence Sam" Johnny stressed. "Now, what is it you want to know?"

"By the way, I love the ringtone on your phone Johnny" Sam said, "you answered the call too quickly for me to work out what it was."

Johnny's phone rings again but one look at who it's from convinces him not to answer. With no voicemail installed, the phone will continue to ring until it is answered or the caller hangs up.

Johnny then grabs his mobile, not to answer the call but to turn up the volume. "The one and only Rolling Stones Sam, Sympathy For The Devil."

Johnny then proceeds to go through the repossession processes with Sam as "Sympathy For

The Devil" continues to play.

https://www.youtube.com/watch?v=GgnClrx8N2k

Chapter 7 Day 1

Two days later the first formal day of Sensitive Matters dawned with Brianna seated at her desk looking bored. Logan and Mary were glued to their screens while Sam was analysing the latest arrears index. The clock has just passed 10 o'clock, two hours since Sensitive Matters officially commenced and the team was yet to take a telephone call.

"I did eventually warm to the idea of doing something with a little less pressure and slower than what I encountered as a Hardship team leader but not this slow," Brianna whined as she viewed a website, www.haveareunion.com where she was sent an invitation to join her former school pals for a fifteen-year reunion.

"Suits me fine" Logan, who is seated at the desk next to her, responded. "Gives me more time to check out the waves" as he scours the internet. "Though I kinda miss the madness of Late Arrears."

Mary is using the spare time to read the training modules Sam provided to each of them on vulnerable clients.

"You could utilise the time" Mary remarked, "to learn about sensitive matters from these modules"

"Already read them" Logan retorted.

"I don't need to read them" Brianna reacted, "After three years as a team leader in Hardship and Financial Assistance I know everything there is to know about vulnerable clients."

"Actually Bree" Mary added "with all your Hardship knowledge and experience, you could give us some training."

"It's not my job to train you" Brianna reacted while looking at Sam.

Sam felt he needed to tread carefully. He knew Brianna had struggled in Hardship, but not due to regulatory knowledge—if anything, she was an expert on compliance. The real issue was people management. The HR reports Bulldog had shared made it clear: Brianna lacked empathy, had three ongoing bullying complaints, and held the highest attrition rate of any leader in the bank. Yet, despite these challenges she presented, Sam believed she had a strong work ethic, and her expertise in hardship cases, an area in which he lacked detailed knowledge, would be invaluable.

"That will give you more time to make one of your famous chocolate cakes," Sam said lightly.

"Though Mary does have a point."

Meanwhile, in meeting room 4.41, Gavin and Stuart analysed the latest arrears index.

"Point seven four," Gavin muttered. "Highest in seven years."

"Coding more accounts to Sensitive Matters will help," Stuart reasoned. "Frees us to go harder on the rest."

"Not to mention a nice drop in complaints." Gavin nodded. "Sam's team takes the heat, while we do what we do best."

"A hundred accounts to agents yesterday," Stuart reported. "Same today."

"Repossessions?" Gavin asked.

""70-30" responded Stuart. "70% are to take the car - keys over cash. We're going in hard. I've told Johnny Kep to give us an update on the garage on Monday"

"The garage" is what Late Arrears describe for the vehicles which have been repossessed and to be prepared for public auction. It's loved by Gavin and his team because once the vehicle is sold and the proceeds are credited to the loan, the remaining debt goes from being secured against the vehicle to unsecured, now that there is no asset attached.

These debts are then charged off the books and removed from the balance sheet. The loan balance is crystallised and interest is frozen however the debt remains due and payable by the client, who is then pursued by a separate Global team, known as "Loss Recovery". Most importantly, in Gavin's eyes, they are no longer a live account so do not get included in the arrears index.

Gavin smiled. He dialled Johnny Kep. "Meet me in 4.41," he ordered before turning back to Stuart. "We have two hundred cars. Seventy percent commercial."

Stuart grinned. "Garage is about to double."

Consumer loans are a bane to hardened and seasoned collections folk because they are regulated by the National Consumer Credit Protection Act (NCCP), commercial loans are not.

The NCCP affords consumers a range of protections, including 28 days to pay the overdue debt before the vehicle may be sold. If the loan is 75% paid, the lender requires a court order to repossess the vehicle, an expensive process which is rarely adopted due to the costs involved. Commercial contracts don't have these reprieves and Gavin and Stuart pull out all stops to take advantage.

Johnny arrived, sporting freshly dyed jet-black hair. Gavin smirked. "What happened to the greys, Johnny?"

"New look," Johnny said simply.

Johnny's love for photography, surfing and healthy eating and disdain for alcohol ensures he keeps in good shape much to the chagrin of Gavin and Stuart who are the opposite of Johnny in almost every way. Johnny keeps things close to his chest, especially his private life which is a reason he is not part of The Club - Gavin doesn't think he can control him. So while there is a mutual distrust, Gavin has a lofty respect for Johnny's work ethic, astute knowledge of car prices and his meticulous management of the garage.

Back at Sensitive Matters

The phones finally rang. Brianna consoled a widow whose husband had just passed. Logan, however, looked increasingly concerned "Alice, I'm really sorry," Logan said, gripping his headset. "Let me speak to my manager."

Sam was nearby and had been listening to Logan speak. Though he has the telephony tools to listen into live calls, he chose not to on this occasion and only heard the conversation from Logan's perspective but he sensed it was serious.

"Alice Rhodes, a seventy-two-year-old on a disability pension. We've just repossessed her car." Logan sighed. "She's in tears."

Mary frowned. "Why are we lending to pensioners?"

"She was 65 when the loan was taken out" Logan responded "and working as a nurse at the time, novated lease."

"Mate" Sam said, "we've dealt with these before, in Late Arrears. If they can't help it's handled by either Hardship or Johnny Kep."

"Already assessed for Hardship. Declined. No capacity to pay," Logan said.

"If it's novated, she must have insurance," Sam reasoned.

"You're right" Logan agreed, but the loan was for five years, as was the term of the insurance cover but she's had a ton of hardship and contract extensions which has led to the loan now ballooning to ten years."

Mary shook her head. "Loan protection insurance is a scam. Clients don't even know they have it or that they have been charged. To the insurance company it's worth thousands but to the poor client it's not worth the paper it's written on."

It dawned on Sam that this is what Sensitive Matters was all about. Whereas previous disputes like this would go to the Complaints team, now they would be referred to him. The buck stops here.

"Lives on her own in outback Queensland, a town by the name of Roma, no public transport and needs to travel to get to medical appointments" Logan elaborated. "The craziest part about all this is the client was getting to the end of the loan, only owes five grand. The cost of sending an agent out to repossess will be in the thousands, just not worth it for such a low balance."

Mary leaned forward. "Wasn't it seventy-five per cent paid?"

"Commercial loan," Logan reminded her. "No consumer protections."

"Of course, silly me," Mary reacted. "Even though, in my view, a novated lease for someone who is an employee of a company should be a consumer loan and covered by the NCCP. Gee, if I were ever to buy a car on finance - which I never would having worked here and seen what goes on - it would be a consumer loan."

One of the conditions of a consumer loan is if it is 75% or more paid, the financier cannot repossess the vehicle without a court order which is a costly process and invariably uneconomical to pursue, whereas commercial contracts are not subjected to this. They, for instance, could be 95% paid and there is no such protection.

"Customer worked as a nurse until she became sick and had to resign." Logan advised. "Hence it's understandably a novated lease."

"So what's your solution Logan?" Sam asked.

"I don't have one Sam" Logan replied, "that's why I'm coming to you."

Sam stood there pondering the options. When he was team leader of Collections, anytime a car was repossessed was a time to celebrate. They now held the upper hand and the only way the vehicle would be returned is when all the arrears, plus agent's costs were paid. Rarely did this happen resulting in the asset being sold at public auction "We can't just give the car back," Sam said.

"That's exactly what we can do," Mary shot back.

"Not until she pays the arrears and agent's bill" Sam added.

The frustration Mary had suffered was now turning to anger. She kept a keen eye on the events as they unfolded, both in listening to Logan on the phone and his subsequent conversation with Sam.

"She doesn't have any money Sam" Mary thundered. "She is 72 years old, not an asset or cent to her name, is unwell and needs to regularly see a doctor and desperately needs this car."

"Gosh you know more about the client than Logan" Brianna quipped, having finished her own discussion with a separate, vulnerable client.

"OK" Sam offered, "I'll tell you what we do. The client only has to pay the arrears, we'll waive the agent's costs."

"What part of "doesn't have a cent" do you not understand Sam?" Mary snapped. She's old, sick, broke. She needs that car to survive."

Back in 4.41

"Pymbles auction Friday. Twenty-five cars," Johnny reported.

"That's the one we'll be at," Stuart added.

"Got to remind Jimmy to order low-carb beers this time," Gavin remarked, feeling his tummy.

Sam burst in. "Gents, we have an issue. Johnny, do we have a recently repossessed Toyota Landcruiser?"

Johnny checked his notes. "Roma, Queensland. Auction reserve is twenty-two grand."

"May have to withdraw or postpone for a later date, "Sam said, "client just rang in, she's in a real state."

"Consumer or Commercial?" Gavin asked.

"Commercial. Novated lease," Sam confirmed.

Gavin scoffed. "Why would we withdraw?"

"A seventy-two-year-old. Medical issues. Lives in the middle of nowhere," Sam explained.

"So?" Stuart shrugged. "We hear sob stories every day."

"Can she pay?" Johnny asked.

"Nope," Sam admitted. "not anytime soon anyway. She has no money or assets for that matter, the car is her only possession."

The car is not the client's possession" Gavin reacted before crossing his arms, "the car belongs to us until it's paid out and if the customer doesn't pay, the vehicle is repossessed. The car sells as scheduled."

Sam clenched his jaw. "Understood."

"This is your baby now Sam," Gavin stressed, "dealing with all the "vulnerable" clients.

Though in this particular case I fail to see how she fits into this category. Irrespective, I put you in charge because you are the best man for the job. Smooth it over with the client, I'm sure you will know what to say."

"And we have the upper hand" Stuart added, "with the vehicle in the garage we hold the trump card. If we give it back our leverage is gone."

"Yeah" Sam sighed, "of course you are right, I'll take care of it" as he turned and left the room.

Back at his desk, Logan and Mary waited. Sam returned.

"No go," he said. "Unless she pays the arrears, the car goes to auction tomorrow."

Chapter 8 Skip-Tracers

The following Friday morning, in Parramatta - a thriving suburb in Sydney's west and about 25 kilometres from Manly - the head office of Scholes & Sons is abuzz with activity.

Scholes & Sons is Australia's leading mercantile agency, employing over 250 people nationwide and specialising in vehicle repossession for finance companies. Renowned for their ruthless efficiency, they excel in persuading debtors to pay their arrears and in locating those who have seemingly vanished— referred to in the industry as "skips." Their dedicated skip-tracing team is particularly esteemed for tracking down clients with whom financial institutions have lost contact.

The energy in the office was palpable as the four members of the skip-tracing team, all present and engaged, revelled in their latest successes in locating wayward debtors. Scholes' skip-tracing specialists worked six days a week, with Saturdays being their most productive day. Many debtors, or those who might assist in locating them, tended to be more accessible at the weekend. However, Fridays were also favoured, as the team believed that people often let their guard down on the last working day of the week.

Skip tracing is treated by many in the mercantile industry as a work of art, a science, which requires intelligence, acumen, a highly competitive nature and boldness. Scholes' biggest customer is The Global bank and their team of four takes great pride in finding debtors which Global couldn't.

At 8:30 am, Billy Barnes, a 64-year-old industry veteran, was deep into his second hour at his desk, scouring the internet. His three colleagues—Rod Weller, Angus Wangle, and Mo Angel—were already on the phones, making outbound calls, eagerly waiting for someone to pick up.

"I think I've got something for Jacka" Billy murmured Rod and Angus both instantly and simultaneously hung up their phones, keen to know what Billy had uncovered while Mo stayed on the line after successfully making contact.

"Oh hi, is this Robert Hardaker?" Mo enquired. The response was only audible to Mo but it soon becomes evident what he was told, while two desks over Billy unveiled his latest discovery to Angus and Rod.

"A Facebook post from a friend of a friend of a friend indicates Ronald Jacka is at Mclean Hospital Mental Health Facility" Billy evinced.

"My humblest apologies" Mo grovelled, "I thought this was 19 Auburn Street but you are telling me you are at number 21?"

After another response from the recipient Mo steps into gear. This is a common tactic employed by the Scholes skip-tracers when endeavouring to determine a debtor's whereabouts - calling related or third parties. While field agents could be dispatched for an in-person visit, such operations were costly and often fruitless. Telephone inquiries were a far more economical method.

The team routinely contacted neighbours, relatives, work colleagues, or anyone likely to provide useful information. In this instance Mo contacted the next-door neighbour.

"That is very accommodating of you ma'am, yes I would love you to pass a message to Mr Hardaker. Would you ask him to telephone Mo at Scholes Mercantile on 02 9455 5555."

"Ezitrace strikes again," Angus beamed, "that search engine is worth every penny Scholes pays for it."

Meanwhile, Billy has found the McLean Hospital's contact details. Without hesitation, he picked up the phone and dialled the number.

"Hello, this is Billy Barnes, is this the mental health wing of Mclean Hospital?" Billy paused as the other end responded.

"That's great. I've just heard one of my best friends has been admitted there and I want to send him a gift and let him know I am thinking of him and there for him" Billy continued smoothly.

He listened intently before adding: "his name is Ronald Jacka, great guy for whom I feel the utmost sympathy."

Rod and Angus edged closer to Billy's desk. Ronald Jacka has a Ford Ranger under finance, the loan of which is $20k in arrears. There have been no payments in over a year and nobody at the bank or Scholes has spoken to him in more than 10 months. To them, finding Ronald -and more importantly the Ford Ranger - will be a massive victory.

"Well thanks for confirming that" Billy said smilingly, "take care and have a great day."

As Billy hung up, Ron and Angus leaned in eagerly.

"He's there all right, we've got him" Billy beamed

Rod pumped his fist as the trio exchanged high-fives, celebrating another successful find.

"Of course we don't know the Ranger is parked at the hospital so we need to proceed cautiously but I am pretty confident that it is," Billy said.

"Let's get Cosimo on the case" Angus declared, send him out there now. If that car is there, we want it out of there pronto."

Cosimo is Scholes' top repossession agent and as Billy dialled the number, an incoming call rang on Scholes' main line, which Rod quickly answered.

"Scholes, this is Rod, how can I help you?"

Another of their standard tactics was to withhold the full company name when answering calls.

Many debtors, receiving unidentified SMS messages, would ring out of curiosity. The moment they realised they were speaking to a repossession agency, they often hung up. However, when leaving messages for third parties, the team deliberately included the full name—Scholes Mercantile—so the recipient assumed the debtor's financial issues had been disclosed to an external party, often prompting them to act.

"Oh sure" Rod replied "I can transfer you to Mo. May I ask who is calling?"

He paused then nodded knowingly.

"One minute please Mr Hardaker."

Mo had heard everything and grinned. His strategy with the neighbour worked. He signalled to

Rod he was ready to take the call.

"Hello, Mr Hardaker, this is Mo. Thank you for calling—"

But before he could continue, Hardaker launched into a furious tirade, his shouting audible across the office. Mo remained unfazed, patiently waiting for a break in the verbal onslaught.

"I did not tell your neighbour I want to repossess your car Mr Hardaker" Mo interrupted coolly, "nor did I tell them you have a debt with us, you only assumed that. Though now that we are on the topic, you do owe ....."

Two desks to Mo's right, Billy is about to hang up his phone after successfully engaging Cosimo to repossess the Ford Ranger from the mental health facility.

"Gotcha" Billy says gleefully. "Sunny is coming home."

It was an inside joke among the Scholes skip-tracers, a nod to Shawn Colvin's song Sunny Came Home. While the lyrics bore no connection to repossession, the team had adopted the phrase as a metaphor—the asset was returning to its rightful owner.

Over at Global's Manly office Mary was flourishing in her new role. In Collections the focus was always on extracting payments, regardless of a client's financial reality - something about which she was often uncomfortable. But In Sensitive Matters her objective is in finding ways to help the client, an approach she found far more rewarding. Mary would leave no stone unturned in learning every aspect of the client's situation, ensuring she was thoroughly across everything before making a case to Sam.

"Ingrid Pavlich" Mary said as Sam stood alongside, peering at her computer as she sat at her desk. "Six months in arrears, agents have been instructed to repossess, loan bal is $45,000 with the vehicle valued at $30k."

"Um" Sam reacted, "remember what today is?"

"Sorry" Mary said, "the loan balance."

"What is so special about today?" Bree enquired.

"It's No Abbreviation Day (NAD)" Logan advised, "one day a month we must not abbreviate any words, we have to say them in full. Sam's idea when we were in Collections. Weren't allowed to say 'NOD' for example, had to be Notice of Demand, helped to appreciate the meaning a bit more."

"No NOD on a NAD" Bree quipped.

"What is the category?" Sam asked, returning to the discussion with Mary.

"Terminal illness" Mary replied. "Ingrid is a mother of four school-aged children, unable to work due to suffering from cancer and being paralysed from the waist down and lives in country Victoria, with the nearest hospital over 2 hours away."

"Is she married?" Sam asks.

"Yes" Mary responds, aware the reason Sam asked this was to understand the household income, "but her husband was forced to quit his job to become Ingrid's full-time carer. The vehicle was also specially modified to include her wheel-chair-"

"Did she get our permission to modify the vehicle," Sam interjected, "as per the terms and conditions of the contract?"

Mary didn't respond, bringing a sigh from Sam. In Collections quick solutions were relatively simple: cash or keys. But he knew Mary wouldn't come to him if either of these options were viable.

"So what are you proposing?" Sam quizzed.

"The doctor's reports are looking better and Ingrid has shown some improvement indicating there are positive signs she will get through this. I think we give her 12 months of no payments, after which she will hopefully be in a position for either her or her husband to return to work and resume repayments."

"Twelve months!" Sam reacted, "that will go down like a lead balloon with Bulldog. The first thing he thinks of is the arrears index - which is too high as it is - and if we allow a loan to fall eighteen months in arrears the index will worsen. Not to mention a terrible precedent would have been set."

Brianna was listening to the conversation and knew there was another option, thanks to her Hardship experience. She was a little hesitant to get involved as her dismay at changing roles had not waned but realised Mary's proposal would falter.

"We could capitalise the arrears Sam" Brianna interjected, "put the arrears to the end of the loan and make her next rental payment due in 12 months. That would not impact the index."

"I appreciate that Bree" Sam responded "but it would have an impact on provisioning and money taken off the balance sheet which cannot be used for lending. And with all the accrued interest the balance would skyrocket and put the client in a worse position, even if - and it's a big if - she recovers and returns to work in 12 months. By repossessing and selling the asset now, the loss will be far less than in 12 months when the balance would be much higher and the value of the vehicle less due to depreciation."

"But we can't take back the car Sam" Mary implored.

"Yes we can" Sam replied "but look" as his tone became more empathetic, "let me look over the doctors' reports before any decision is made" as he walked back to his desk. "And if it comes to it, I am more than happy to ring Ingrid myself and explain why surrendering the vehicle is the best

Option."

As he sat down Sam noticed a flash on his mobile phone, a reminder that Vincent will be in the school play in three days, an event Sam assured Abbey he would attend.

The towie

Thirty kilometres from Manly, travelling along the New South Wales Hume highway is a burly,

middle-aged male with jet-black, curly hair and clad in a hi-vis yellow vest and sunglasses, driving a truck, towing a Ford Ranger.

The driver sings along to the song on the radio, Shawn Colvin's "Sunny Came Home".

Sunny Came Home

Chapter 9 The Burrow

A week is a long time in politics, so the cliche goes, and the same can be stated for Sensitive Matters, with cases pouring in at an alarming rate.

Into its second week, the atmosphere on this unseasonably warm Spring Monday morning was the polar opposite of a week earlier. The team had quickly discovered that even the slightest mention of mental illness or feeling low to a customer service or collections agent was enough to have the contract immediately coded to Sensitive Matters. Upon investigation, Sam found that the Key Performance Indicators (KPIs) assigned to these other teams had been modified and, whether intentionally or not, now incentivised collections and customer service staff to pass such cases over to Sensitive Matters rather than attempt to resolve them themselves. The advantage for them was clear—it reduced their individual customer portfolios, a major KPI, effectively rewarding them for doing less. Anything even remotely difficult was being shifted to Sensitive Matters.

"Gee whiz" Logan bemoaned, as he leaned back in his chair at his desk, "my portfolio went up by 24 contracts in one day. Are we sure Workflow has given us the correct list Sam?"

"Sensitive Matters increased by 77 contracts over the weekend" Sam revealed, "you could say overnight as it was from Friday. Workflow have got it right. I checked each and every one of the contracts which were coded to us."

"Sorry I'm late" Mary blurts as she walks in the door, scurrying past Sam to her desk.

"Officially you don't start today until 8.45" Sam responded "so one could argue you are ten minutes early." "I like to get here by at least 8 every morning" Mary responded, "you know that."

"I do Mary" Sam beamed, "I love your work ethic."

"Well is there any chance" Logan interjected "you can use that good work ethic to take a few of my contracts?"

"Sure Logan," Mary replied.

"No," Sam interjected, "we stick to the alpha split."

"I was kidding Sam" Logan voiced, "of course I'll do my own. Though there is one here I am sure Mary will like, referred to us from Late Arrears."

This piqued Mary's interest as she rose from her chair and looked over Logan's shoulder at his computer.

"Hats off to our Late Arrears colleagues" Logan praised, there's a heap of information here, including the merc agent's report. Normally we have to wait at least two weeks to get that."

Mary's interest was gaining as she peered into Logan's computer, inadvertently nudging his shoulder, prompting him to stand.

"You know what" Logan politely exclaimed. "This is a good time to visit the TAB. Does anyone want anything?"

"No thanks mate" Sam replied as he wandered over to join Mary who was engrossed in the new referral before turning back to Logan.

"On second thought" Sam mused, "hit me with a daily double will you."

"I'll read through it from my desk," Mary advised as she wrote down the contract number.

"You can keep reading from my computer Mary"; Logan reassured.

"Better not" Sam intervened, "don't want the risk of security poking their noses in and thinking they found something that isn't there." Logan left as Mary brought up the contract on her computer.

"Another case of domestic violence Sam" Mary solemnly revealed as she reviewed the details.

"Tara Baldwin, married for 20 years to Danny Baldwin, they have four children together"

Mary continued, "they bought a house together and each ran their own, successful small businesses in

Bundaberg, Queensland. Tara ran a dance studio while her husband maintained a carpentry company."

Sam returned to his desk as Mary continued reading. The details revealed this was Tara's second contract after she traded in a Ford Territory for a Kia Carnival to accommodate their sizeable family plus to transport gear used for Tara's business.

The Ford Territory lost much of its value and after a trade-in there was still another $5,000 shortfall on the original loan. Tara learned that Global was prepared to add the shortfall onto the new contract and though the interest rate was slightly higher than other banks, the attraction of consolidating it all into the one loan was compelling.

Mary stopped reading Late Arrears' summary and decided to review the account for herself.

She examined the payment history and observed the first 4 years went swimmingly. On two occasions there were missed payments but each time Tara would be on the front foot to ring Global and, apologetically, arrange to bring the contract back up to date.

Then, four years and six months into the loan, the pattern changed. Late payments were more frequent while no calls were made to the bank. Global's attempts to contact Tara would also go unanswered. The payments that were remitted dwindled until it reached the point where the contract ballooned to falling six months into arrears, prompting Global to engage mercantile agents for repossession.

Mary then extracted the agent's report - or reports as she soon discovered the multiple visits undertaken by Scholes. The first visit was telling. The agent knocked on the door and met with a "burly, unshaven male" - Danny. He claimed Tara had moved to an address of which he was unaware though believed it may be in Sydney and her phone number had changed.

Two weeks later, another Scholes' agent visited a new address in Sydney, following a lead from the skip tracing team. The Kia Carnival parked in the driveway suggested they were in the right place.

Mercantile agents have many strings to their bow and one is they are trained to recognise vulnerabilities and on this occasion, upon attending the premises, the agent sensed all was not well.

The overgrown lawn, children's toys strewn across the nature strip and front yard and the vehicle's poor condition painted a concerning picture.

When Tara answered the door, she appeared drawn, with dark circles under her eyes and her hair tied back in a bun. The agent introduced himself as representing Global Car Loans.

This time, Tara's story differed from her previous explanations. She had cited "health issues" as the reason for her arrears, insisting they were temporary and that she would soon be back on track. Now, she admitted she was drowning in debt, struggling to meet basic living expenses for herself and her children. She had recently been forced to close her dance studio due to financial instability.

Tara confessed that she desperately wanted to speak to the bank but had been paralysed by fear—fear of losing the car she relied on to take her children to school and activities. The agent realised the situation was far more complex than an overdue loan.

He picked up his phone and rang the bank before excusing himself and walking to the front lawn. He spoke to the Late Arrears agent who, after learning of the client's plight, told the agent to cease action and inform the client her loan will now be managed by our Sensitive Matters team.

Meanwhile, Logan strolled across The Corso and into the TAB—or as emblazoned on the window, the Tea and Biscuits café, a venue well known to locals. Logan planned to grab a cup of tea and watch some sport on one of the many screens while he waited. The café was themed around its acronym, TAB, with framed photographs of horse racing and major sporting events adorning the walls.

However, unlike its namesake, there was no betting here. Logan is a regular and always glances admiringly at his favourite picture: former world surfing champion, Layne Beechley riding a Manly wave to success in the 1999 Diet Coke Surfwater Classic, the same year she won one of her seven world surfing titles.

There was a queue at the counter, so feeling peckish, Logan browsed the menu:

TRIFECTA – A cup of Irish or English Breakfast tea, a ham, cheese, and tomato toastie, and an ice cream cone.

DAILY DOUBLE – A cup of Irish or English Breakfast tea and two Anzac biscuits.

WIN AND PLACE – A cup of Irish or English Breakfast tea and a double chocolate chip cookie.

"Hi Logan," Carla Ihly, the amiable cafe attendant greeted.

"Hey Carla, "Logan replied, "I came here all set to have the Quinella but you know what, let's go with a Win And Place."

"How much do you want to put on the Win?" Carla asked, "Small, Medium or Large?"

"Well it's definitely not a small one today Carla" Logan reacted, "or a medium for that matter.

Sensitive Matters is going gang busters so you'd better make it a large."

As Carla plucked a take-away cup Logan had second thoughts.

Actually Carla" Logan said, "I just remembered "Sam wants a Daily Double so forget the Win And Place and make it two Daily Doubles."

"Of course" Carla responded, "Irish Breakfast and two Anzacs."

"You know Sam well," Logan acknowledged.

"It just happens to be my favourite daily double too Logan" Carla smiled "most opt for English Breakfast in their DD but I have a soft spot for the Irish."

"Though in my case I will have the English breakfast" Logan said.

Over in the busking area, directly opposite the TAB, an attractive, slender lady in her mid-twenties with long brown hair, is showing some sheet music to a fellow busker about a song they are planning on performing,

The Beatles' "Help" but covering the version released by one of her favourite singers, Johnny Farnham.

Standing a few metres behind The Burrow is Paddy who is chatting to an unfamiliar face to Logan, an older male looking to be in his mid-forties, clad in a black singlet, shorts and an Akubra hat.

They also appear to have a lot of guests. Mingling with them are seven young, fit looking, Maori males, all dressed in black tracksuits. They have all captured Logan's - and numerous others' - eye.

While waiting for his daily double, Logan dashes over to greet Paddy.

"Hey Paddy" Logan greeted, "looks like you have quite a party today."

"We have a special show today, Logan," Paddy revealed, "at about 12.30, bang in the middle of lunch.

Make sure you let Sam and Mary know. And anyone else for that matter."

Logan looks at the chap in the Akubra hat. "Someone new?"

The chap hears this and immediately looks around and extends his hand to Logan, "Ronnie Galah me ol china, charmed to meet you."

"Hi Ronnie" Logan replied, "I'm Logan Johnstone" as he looks slightly perplexed which is noticed by Paddy.

"It's rhyming slang Logan" Paddy explained, "he's not saying you are Chinese, rather me ol' mate, me ol china plate - me ol china."

"Right," Logan said, "makes perfect sense. Look, we are getting smashed at work so not sure if we can all make it to your show but you can be certain Sam will be here with bells on."

"Oh yeah me ol china" Ronnie said, "what do you do for a crust?"

"I work for a bank, Ronnie" Logan replied, "in fact I recently started a new role, in a team which looks after our vulnerable clients, called Sensitive Matters."

Ronnie nodded appreciatively, "Sensitive Matters eh, sounds like a good gig. You must be a cool coot Logan, helping the vulnerable. Because if it is sensitive, it matters."

"That's a good one Ronnie" Logan said, as Carla appeared, armed with a tray carrying the daily doubles."

"Call it a Logan slogan" Ronnie quipped.

"I like that one too," Logan reacted.

"Well mate," Ronnie added, "you'll also like the fact that I've never been on the dole, I've never paid for a root and I've never been engaged."

"Right," Logan said, unsure how to respond to what he saw as a somewhat random comment.

"You can call that a bogan slogan" Carla quipped, "here you go Mr convert, two daily doubles."

"Top of the morning Carla" Paddy greeted, "can I order a quaddie? As you can see we have a few extra mouths to feed."

"Absolutely Paddy" Carla replied, "what's the occasion?"

"You'll find out at 12.30 today" Paddy replied, "spread the word, it will be quite an event."

"See you guys then" Logan remarked as he headed back to the office.

As he departs, Paddy grabs his electric guitar and plays the riff for Michael Jackson's Beat It.

https://www.youtube.com/shorts/BaYDOGikZJ4

Logan stops and turns a little bemused, "are you telling us to beat it?"

Paddy laughs then changes the riff to "Walk This Way" at which Logan points in the direction of the office.

"But make sure you walk back this way at 12.30" Paddy shouted as his guitar playing of Walk This

Way   became   more   pronounced.
https://www.youtube.com/watch?v=xUScFNXAqow

Chapter 10 Ingrid Pavlich

Back in the office, Sam and Mary were engaged in robust conversation.

"All right Mary" Sam frustratingly responded, "Here's what I'll do. We will take back the car and I will waive the agents' costs."

"Sam" Mary responded frustratingly, "this is not dissimilar to the 72 year-old client, Alice. And as I said to you then, your offer will not make one iota of difference. I cannot stress this enough Sam:

Maryanne is a single mother, a victim of domestic violence who desperately needs the car for her and her children."

Logan arrives back with the refreshments and immediately feels the tension in the air.

"Still on that DV case" Logan uttered, "sounds like it could be worse than I thought" as he handed Sam his tea and biscuits.

"It is, way worse Logan" Mary responded, "but we are now onto a different matter, one of mine, Maryanne Jones."

"I appreciate you giving my one a crack Mary, did you come to any conclusions/suggestions?"

Logan queried meekly.

"Nothing yet" Sam responded, "yours is a mess but so is this."

"They all are Sam" Brianna interjected. "I now have 112 cases - every one of them grim."

Brianna was beginning to feel the pressure, as was Mary but her determination to assist the vulnerable helped her to thrive rather than falter. Logan's easy-going nature and propensity for his mind to wander helped him deal with the cases but he too was feeling a little under duress. Sam could sense his team's changing mood, reinforcing the importance he too does not wilt. Not only did he need to be there for his team, he did not want to let Gavin down.

Brianna answered a call as Sam pondered the options. He realised this type of situation was becoming more prevalent and the cash or keys with compassion approach was not a sustainable model.

As Mary stood in silence, staring intently at Sam waiting for an answer, Brianna put her caller on hold.

"Hey Mary, I've got Ingrid Pavlich on the line" Bree announced.

Mary didn't say a word. She left Sam and rushed to her desk. Within seconds the call was transferred and she was speaking to Ingrid.

Sam knew the Ingrid Pavlich situation well. She was one of the first contracts to appear in the Sensitive Matters portfolio and Mary raised this with him a couple of days earlier. Sam read the entire file which revealed that prior to contracting cancer, Ingrid had been a perfect client, never missing a payment. She worked as a teacher at the local school while her husband, Altarf, was an interstate truck-driver. Together they made a sizeable income enabling a comfortable living. When Ingrid was diagnosed she not only had to stop teaching but Altarf, who became her full-time carer, was forced to cease employment as a result.

For six months they used their savings to pay bills, including the car, but when the funds were exhausted, the meagre household income was barely enough to cover essentials, which did not include the car loan. The doctors' reports, of which there were many, gave

Sam little confidence Ingrid would be in a position to return to work in 12 months, even if she survived the cancer. Sam decided that repossessing Ingrid Pavlich's car was the optimum - and only - option, a verdict with which Mary was uncomfortable but accepted. Sam offered to ring Ingrid and personally explain the reasons for the path they would take, to which Mary acceded.

"Did they pick up the vehicle?" Sam asked Brianna. "Don't tell me Ingrid is reneging now on relinquishing the car, I was on the phone to her for an hour on Friday convincing her to which she agreed."

"I think you'd better check in with Mary" Brianna responded, "something appears to have gone amiss."

Sam returned to his desk and dialled in to the phone system to enable him to hear Mary's conversation. Ingrid was very upset and angry at the same time. The repossession agent arrived with a pick-up truck to load the vehicle but after seeing the pristine state of the car, thanks to the pride.

Ingrid's family took in maintaining it, he told her it would be better if someone else were to drive it to the auction house, a 200 kilometre trek.

When Ingrid quizzed why this was necessary the Scholes agent explained he would be personally interested in buying the car at auction and would get his son to test-drive the vehicle. An hour later his son arrived and drove off in the car for a 200 kilometre "test-drive."

Understandably this did not rest well with Ingrid. She felt it was immoral and rubbing salt into the wound. Mary was appalled and reassured Ingrid she would do everything she could to help her, though unsure what that would entail. She ended the call apologetically before storming over to Sam's desk.

"I just got off the phone to Ingrid Pavlich" she announced defiantly, unaware Sam listened to the discussion.

"Great" Sam responded, keen not to divulge he had any knowledge of what transpired. "How did the collection of our asset go?"

"Abysmally" Mary snapped, "actually shocking. The merc agent told her he wants to buy the car at the upcoming auction so arranged for his son to drive it back rather than the standard practice of loading it on a tow-truck."

"So?" Sam reacted.

"So! The poor lady is distraught" Mary responded. "She feels we are taking her for a ride, metaphorically - certainly not literally - and their actions seem so corrupt."

"Look Mary', Sam calmly responded, "I agree this is not a good look but it won't affect the actual auction itself. The agent will not be getting a special deal and will need to bid for the vehicle like everyone else. Besides, as part of the arrangement I made with Ingrid, if the vehicle sells for less than the valuation - to which she agreed - we will wear the difference. If there is a shortfall after the sale, interest will be frozen. The agent's conduct is not becoming but being a scoundrel is not against the law."

"Not a good reflection on Global though," Mary replied, a comment to which Sam's instinct was to challenge before quickly realising he could not disagree.

Sam looked at the inbound monitor to see there was a call in the inbound queue. Logan was on the phone to a client and Sam looked up at Mary who knew what he was thinking. Without saying a word she returned to her desk to take the call.

"And look Mary" Sam said softly, "I will ring her back to smooth it over." A steely eyed Mary looked back at Sam as she was about to answer the call. "No thanks Sam, I can handle it."

Logan appeared to be flummoxed, struggling with the caller's concerns.

"I am sorry but I have never heard of that" Logan said, "I just don't think it's possible." Logan continued to listen. "I'll tell you what I can do Sandie" Logan offered, "I will take this to my manager and run this by him then get back to you."

Sam was doing his best to appear disinterested which was how he felt, enthusiasm waned after his talk with Mary but Logan's comments pricked Bree's ears as Logan ended the call.

"That sounded like a difficult call," Brianna said.

"Not so much difficult Bree," Logan replied, "more like impossible. Sandie Chan, a co-borrower wants her name removed from the loan, she insisted a financial counsellor told her it's possible."

"Well as we know, financial counsellors are usually very thorough" Brianna responded, "so there may be something in that."

"That's why I said I'd speak to Sam" Logan replied.

"Or you can look it up Logan" Mary chimed in as she put her phone on mute while listening to her client.

Two hours later, outside the office building on the Manly Corso a crowd is gathering in the busking area. Brianna decided she will be the one to miss the event and stay logged into the phones to take any inbound calls. 12.20 ticks by and Sam, Mary and Logan head to the lift on their way to The Burrow.

Passing the skybox, they saw Eric presenting to a group, standing before a large wallboard marked KANBAN. Beneath it, Sensitive Matters Team was printed in smaller text. Sam took note but kept walking. Right now, they had one question—what had Paddy planned for them?

The trio stride past the Staines and head to The Burrow. As they approach, Logan notices the seven Maoris have replaced their black tracksuits with traditional Maori garb. They also appear to have their bodies and faces painted.

"What's going on, mate?" Sam asked a nearby spectator.

"The All Blacks are in town bro" the male responded, "playing the Wallabies at the Sydney Football Stadium tomorrow."

Logan overheard the conversation. "I thought those guys looked familiar," Logan blurted,

"they're All Blacks."

Paddy waves to Sam, beckoning him to come over. He then plays a few chords on his guitar before stopping when Sam arrived. "I've gotta be quick mate" Paddy said "but I want you to meet my cousin, Sherese Murray down here from Alice Springs for a few weeks."

A smiling Sherese, a young, slender lady in her mid-twenties with long brown hair, emerged from behind Paddy and extended her hand for her and Sam to shake but Sam was having none of it.

"Gee whiz" Sam blurted, "when it comes to Paddy's cousin, you are family. This doesn't warrant a handshake, it's time for a hug" as they warmly embrace.

"And this is her partner and one of my best mates, Ti" Paddy added as a striking-looking, thickly-set fellow, a millimetre shy of 6 feet tall in his late twenties and appearing to not have an ounce of fat on him emerged.

"Hey Sam" Ti greeted as they also embraced, "Paddy has told me a lot about you, I hear you play a mean guitar."

"And I hear you play a mean didgeridoo" Sam responded before noticing the shirt Ti was wearing with the words "Be Inspired - Make Music" emblazoned across the front. "I like the shirt."

"It's my own 'T-shirt' range," Ti replied, "get it, 'T' shirt. "

Paddy begins playing his guitar in earnest. "Told you this had to be quick" he said to Sam who hastily returns to the large crowd, rejoining Mary and Logan.

Paddy plays the riff of The Eagles' "Life In The Fast Lane" and continues for about twenty seconds.

https://www.youtube.com/watch?v=hnY73K23yGs

He then takes to the microphone.

"Welcome everybody to this special edition of the Buskers' Burrow" Paddy greeted. "Today we have some very special guests, all the way from New Zealand. Here to perform a very famous Maori dance are my Kiwi brothers. So please give a warm welcome as they get set to perform The Haka.

The crowd cheers as the seven Maori males launch into a rousing rendition of "The Haka".

After finishing their performance the seven All Blacks surrounded a microphone stand as Paddy and Ti remained in their positions while Sherese approached her microphone.

"As part of our joint performance, our Kiwi brothers are joining us to perform one of my favourites. The Kiwis then start singing the opening lines of Yothu Yindi's "Djapana".

https://www.youtube.com/watch?v=aMX2PrHPXzY

Chapter 11 Tara Baldwin

The next day dawned and in Sam's mind, they needed a new approach. He could see the toll dealing solely with vulnerable clients was starting to take on his team and sought to reduce some of the intensity. While he still had his misgivings about the whole concept of Sensitive Matters and treating vulnerable clients differently, he had no such reservations about the wellbeing of his team. In Sam's mind they always came first.

The large whiteboard, which is the first thing anyone sees when venturing into the Sensitive Matters domain, would normally display the team's daily and weekly statistics plus the latest figures of the arrears index. Sam decided to retain the weekly figures, index, and daily numbers but made room to add:

Song of the Week - John Mayer - No Such Thing

Musical of the Week - West Side Story

Special Guest of the Week - Paul Keating

Sam looked at the whiteboard then at his team to see Brianna on the phone to a vulnerable client and Logan preparing to answer the call in the queue before striding towards them singing, "Welcome to the real world....."

https://www.youtube.com/watch?v=H1W2UddURXI

Logan desisted from answering the phone and looked up at Sam who stopped singing, smiled and said, "Song of the week".

Mary was less than three feet from Sam and Logan but didn't hear or see any of their interaction. Her eyes were glued to her computer screen. That was not unusual for Mary but being at her desk in the office at 7 o'clock was. It was now 9.30 a.m. and Mary had spent the entire 2 and a half hours fixated on her portfolio, not even a break for a glass of water. But it wasn't just her portfolio on which Mary was focused; a sizeable chunk of her morning, such was her innately caring attitude, was spent reviewing the case of Tara Baldwin.

Though this contract was in Logan's portfolio, Mary was intent on doing whatever she could to help this victim of domestic violence. The most recent mercantile agent report, the one which resulted in the case being referred to Sensitive Matters, noted Tara was a different person when her husband, Danny, was not around. Mary was surprised - and impressed - by how well the agent dealt with Tara. It was clear the agent adopted a different approach to the norm where standard practice was to repossess the car, load it onto the two-truck, and ask questions later. On this occasion, the agent showed a distinct concern for her wellbeing. Mary believed it was this display of compassion, patience and empathy that led to Tara opening up about her predicament. Despite dozens of conversations with Global representatives and mercantile agents in the past, this was the first time Tara mentioned she was a victim of domestic violence. She revealed, that despite there being an Apprehended Violence Order (AVO) against Danny, she was forced to flee with her children and move to another state.

Danny made life even more difficult for Tara by failing to pay child support, pleading poverty despite running two successful businesses, and, since the break-up, buying a brand new Harley Davidson motorcycle.

Agents have a tendency to add their personal views when writing their report and this one was no exception, penning "the ex-husband has made shifting money around an art-form". Mary took stock. Tara had gone from owning her own home in a city in which she had lived for twenty years and running her own business to fleeing to another state, renting a run-down house and working part-time stacking shelves for a local supermarket. Tara also approached charities for food hampers to feed her children and as the sole carer, losing the car was definitely not an option.

Mary decided to go back to the beginning and review the loan application. It revealed the purchase price for the Kia Carnival was $29,499 and in the four-and-a-half years since inception, Tara had paid a total of $49,000. But there was still a balance owing of $12,000. Mary was well aware that Global Car Loans interest rates were, at times, relatively high, plus there was the $5,000 shortfall after the trade-in, but to end up the purchase price didn't make sense.

Page 22 of the loan application proved to be telling. A range of insurances, exceeding $12,000 had been added to the loan. This put the real purchase price at over $41,000 because Global always factored insurance premiums into the interest rate. This meant that without the insurances Tara would've incurred the base rate of 8.5% but with the premiums now included, the interest rate ballooned to 12.1%.

Tara wouldn't be the first client to not understand how this worked and while Mary didn't know one way or the other, she suspected Tara was never properly informed at the time she purchased the car. Especially, as in Mary's eyes, the insurances provided were essentially useless with no logical prospect of ever being utilised.

There was $5,800 loan protection insurance which can cover employees working for a company and those who are self-employed but the latter clause was deleted, rendering it pointless for Tara. There was $2800 for "Shortfall insurance" which covers the borrower in the event the vehicle is repossessed and sold and the proceeds fail to cover the balance of the loan. The insured is not then liable for the shortfall which is paid by the insurance company. However, Tara needed the vehicle for her family and business and such a scenario was highly improbable, not to mention impractical.

Mary's concentration is broken by Sam who approaches still singing the song of the week: "I

wanna run through the halls of my school, I wanna scream at the top of my lungs-"

"Good Sam" Mary interjected, "I wanna scream at the top of my lungs too. About Tara Baldwin."

Sam stops singing and pulls up a chair to sit next to Mary. "You know the case" Mary continues, "and it is one that is really starting to eat at me."

"Well don't let it" Sam reacted unsympathetically. "We used to get difficult cases in Late Arrears too, nowhere near as often, I know, but as I would say then, you cannot get yourself emotionally attached to these clients."

"That is so easy to say, Sam," Mary reacted defiantly, "and way harder - no, it's actually not possible - to do. Since joining this team I have come to the realisation that once we approve a loan we have a responsibility to look after customers that goes beyond good customer service and getting them to pay on time. I could argue that if we didn't approve the loan the vulnerable client would not be in this predicament, so in effect we helped to create it. Yes they may have gone to another bank if we declined them but that's not the point. We contributed to a client's situation, good or bad. Just as we take pride in helping someone buy a home or a car, we need to take pride in helping the vulnerable.

And please don't liken Sensitive Matters to Late Arrears; there is no comparison, chalk and cheese."

Sam accepts Mary's point and nods agreeingly while noticing in the distance Angie, pushing a trolley filled with fruit and loaves of bread heading their way.

"I think we should waive the debt" Mary states emphatically. "Correction. I don't think we should waive the debt, I know we should waive the debt."

Angie is now within a stone's throw of SM and, sensing Sam and Mary are engaged in a serious conversation, is careful not to interrupt them so smiles and waves as she veers towards the kitchen.

Sam is unsure how to respond to Mary so takes the opportunity to give himself some breathing space and makes a dash for the kitchen before quickly returning munching a banana.

"The thing is Mary" Sam resumed, "and I've been meaning to talk to you about this, so now is as good a time as any, but you are taking on way too much, Tara Baldwin is not even in your portfolio." Sam's insensitivity brought a sharp glare from Mary compelling Sam to change tack, conscious of diffusing Mary's intensifying ire.

"What is the balance?" Sam asked.

"It's a little over $12,000" Mary replied, buoyed by Sam now appearing to show empathy, "but when I looked into the loan further, I discovered that the car cost $29k, and to date, Tara has paid back almost fifty thousand dollars."

"Insurance?" Sam asked, in a mocking, state-the-obvious tone, aware of this common car dealership tactic.

"Useless insurance" Mary expressed, "the interest rate went from 8.5% to 12.1% as a result.

Without the insurances, the loan would've been paid out by now."

Sam was not opposed to insurance. He subscribed to the mantra that clients were not forced to take them out and if the client signed for it the client pays for it. But he also knew that loan protection and shortfall insurances were lucrative earners for brokers and dealerships. Shortfall insurance was golden. It only comes into play if a balance remains after the car is written off or stolen and the comprehensive cover fails to meet the loan balance, referred to as an "Insurance Total Loss", something which was a relative rarity.

Logan is in the process of logging out of his computer. Though it is still morning, Logan has taken a half-day of annual leave so he can go surfing. His board leans against the umbrella stand looking like it shares Logan's eagerness to hit the waves.

"Logan" Sam shouts, "before you go, I need to talk to you about something," Logan joins Sam and Mary, aware they were discussing a contract in his portfolio. "Tara Baldwin?" Logan asked, knowing the answer. "I agree," he added.

"Agree with what?" Sam quizzed.

"I agree with Mary; We sing from the same hymn book Bree," Logan replied, "we need to waive this debt."

Sam didn't respond, digesting his surprise at Logan's view. Normally complicit with everything Sam said, this was the first time Logan had taken an opposite stance, made all the more jolting when Logan knew Sam's staunch aversion to waiving debts.

"Look, I know the mere thought of waiving a debt when the client still has the car borders on heresy for you Sam" Logan continued, "but this is a shocking case; this poor lady has been through enough"

Sam leans back in his chair and notices the television screen perched above them to their right is flashing Global's mid-year results - a 14% profit increase on the same period the previous year.

Mary looks at the same screen before giving a wry smile.

"Tara Baldwin's debt will not impact Global in the slightest" Mary asserted, "but it has an enormous impact on her and her children. The $240 rental payment is far better off with Tara and her children than it is with Global Bank."

"I couldn't agree more, Mary and Sam" Logan uttered as he walked over to pluck his surfboard from the umbrella stand before returning. "Now, if you don't mind, I have some waves to catch" as he headed to his desk to pick up his briefcase.

"All right Mary" Sam said, "put everything in an e-mail making your case, and we'll take it to Bulldog and Stuart."

"We?" Mary asked sceptically.

"That's right," Sam replied, "you can join me and we can do this together. I think you make a strong case, so let's see what Bulldog thinks."

Mary smiles and immediately clicks on her e-mail to begin her summary. Logan has now made it out of the office and heads to the beach when he eyes Gavin and Stuart laughing and drinking at The Staines. He also notices Sherese occupying the busker's area, playing the guitar and singing as Paddy supports on drums. As Logan gets closer, he observes Sherese is singing without a microphone which is not required thanks to her strong, distinct and almost contralto voice, some may say a mezzo soprano, and is clearly heard above the instruments. Logan recognises the song, and as he gets closer, he wonders if the song is near the end or midway through.

Sherese then launches into the second stanza of Suzanne Vega's "My Name Is Luka."

https://www.youtube.com/watch?v=8huO5Dqeki4

Chapter 12 Everybody Hurts

Later that day, at 2.55 in the afternoon, Sam, armed with his laptop, walks along the hallway towards room 4.43 where he sees Gavin and Stuart seated at the table. He quickens his step and checks the time to see he is five minutes early for their meeting scheduled to kick off at 3 o'clock.

"Top of the morning gents" Sam says cheerfully as he enters 4.43.

"I'd rather it was bottom of the index" Gavin quipped.

Sam didn't react as he sat at the table and opened his laptop.

"Similarly with these sensitive cases" Gavin added, "the numbers are through the roof."

"Tell me about it" Sam replied, "any time someone has a sniff of sensitivity the contract is coded to us. We're getting swamped."

"Yeah but do they all fall into the sensitive categories?" Stuart asked.

"That's a very good point Stuart" Sam reacted, "a big problem has been Customer Service and Collections sending through contracts willy nilly, many which should not have been coded to us indicating they don't seem to have a proper understanding of what qualifies for a Sensitive Matters referral. So I've put together a process chart for them to follow which, I am confident, will lead to only correct referrals to us."

"That's good Sam" Gavin added "but that is not the purpose of this meeting. I called you in about the index, eighty percent of the contracts in Sensitive are 60 days or more in arrears. Some have gone in excess of twelve months without a payment. At this rate we won't be able to collect because they'll be stat barred."

Sam smiled knowing Bulldog was semi-joking though his hyperbole was intended to emphasise his displeasure at the high level of arrears in Sensitive Matters.

"You think I'm joking Sam," Bulldog said.

"I get your point Bulldog" Sam reacted "but the statute of limitations for debt collection is six years. A

loan has to go six years without a payment before it is statute barred and we must cease collections.

The most overdue contract in Sensitive Matters is fourteen months so that is not going to happen."

"In the Northern Territory it is three years" Stuart interjected.

"And in every other state in Australia it is six years" Sam countered firmly.

Over in the Sensitive Matters domain, Brianna has arrived - late - and is logging into her computer, aware a call has been in queue for twelve minutes with both Logan and Mary on the phone.

She gives a sigh before answering the call.

Back in room 4.43, Gavin and Stuart have continued their attack on the high number of Sensitive Matters loans in arrears, impressing upon Sam of the urgency in engaging repossession agents when it's clear the client is not in a reasonable position to pay. Sam is starting to feel the pressure, and belief, that they don't fully understand how difficult the role is and while he was listening to Bulldog and Stuart spouting the facts and figures he spontaneously thought of an idea to help them understand. Sam proposed to present a two hour meeting every week, revealing challenging cases with the aim to get their input and ensure the correct strategy to deal with these is being adopted.

"………. and I'll call it Sensitive Matters Friday" Sam concluded to an intrigued and attentive.

Gavin and Stuart. As Gavin nods approvingly the door opens. It's Brianna.

"So sorry to bother you Bulldog" Brianna advances, "but I urgently need to speak to Sam."

"That's fine Bree" Gavin replies, "we were finishing up anyway. Good idea Sam regarding Sensitive Matters Friday, I'll look out for the invitation."

Sam, looking perturbed, quickly closed his laptop and joined Brianna as they briskly walked back to their desks.

"I need your approval to collect a car urgently" Brianna urged. "I have the mother of the client on the line, her daughter committed suicide."

"Do we have a copy of the death certificate" Sam asked, "did she leave a will, is the mother-"

"No will and the death certificate is held up due to a coroner's investigation," Brianna replied, "the only asset the client had was the car, a Ford Mustang."

The mention of the make and model prompted Sam to have an immediate flashback to a recent chat with Ali who had provided hardship assistance to a client in a mental facility. His brisk walk turned into a run.

"Let me look at the account," Sam said.

Sam sat at Brianna's desk and pored over the details of the customer, Angela Rankin. He knew it was the same customer whom Ali assisted but struggled to believe it. Why, after only recently being providing with three months assistance, where no payments were required during that period, would

Angela then commit suicide?

Sam looked closer and his heart sank. Ali had agreed to the three-month moratorium but had committed two glaring blunders. Firstly he overlooked coding the account to Hardship and secondly, he failed to properly process the contract change. The result was that hardship assistance was never executed with the contract systematically being returned to Collections.

The Late Arrears agent, in whose portfolio this account appeared, failed to notice the hardship approval and promptly sent the client a Notice Of Demand.

What's the mother's name?" Sam asked.

"Jenny Johannsen," Brianna replied.

Sam pondered the options, concerned that when Angela received the NOD it pushed her over the edge, plus whether or not Jenny was aware of the Hardship bungle.

"So, and this is probably a silly question" Sam said, "but how is Jenny, is she holding up OK?"

"She appears to be holding up pretty well under the circumstances," Brianna replied "Why the urgency?" Sam posed, "can we arrange it to be collected when Scholes has an agent in the area?"

"The sight of the car causes her grief," Brianna explained "She would like to see the car gone as soon as possible as it reminds her of her daughter. It turns out the only reason Angela bought the Mustang was because it was her father's favourite car but he never had the money to buy one."

"Oh really" Sam said becoming more buoyant, "does he want the car then" Sam asked, "We have a lot of generous options which I am sure he'd find very appeal-"

"He passed away last year" Brianna interjected, "also suicide. Jenny said Angela left a note that she will now be with her dad which seems to have given some comfort."

At that moment Johnny Kep made an appearance.

"Had lunch yet Sam" Johnny asked "Not yet Johnny" Sam responded, "gotta deal with this challenging case first."

"I thought all sensitive matters cases were challenging" Johny quipped, "what's with this one?"

Sam, I need to get back to Mrs Johannsen" Brianna interrupted, "is it approved?"

"Of course" Sam nodded, "get onto Scholes to arrange collection."

"Client passed away," Sam replied to Johnny, as Brianna resumed speaking to Jenny Johannsen. "Suicide. We are speaking to the mother now."

"What sort of car is it?" Johnny quizzed.

"A Ford Mustang" Sam replied.

"Great" Johnny reacted, "they tend to sell real well and we have the perfect auction coming up in a couple of weeks."

"I'll keep you posted," Sam said.

"So when you say suicide" Johnny added, "the client didn't die in the vehicle did she?"

"No idea" Sam sighed, "there is still plenty to digest."

"We had a case a year ago" Johnny added, "where the client died in a car crash and the vehicle was a write-off but the insurance company wouldn't pay out claiming the driver crashed it deliberately to die by suicide."

"How'd it end up?" Sam asked.

"Still fighting them," Johnny replied. "Porsche, hundred and fifty grand, estate had nothing."

"Let's do lunch tomorrow Johnny" Sam said, "if that's all right with you. I have a few pressing cases which require urgent attention but let's catch up at the TAB."

Johnny saluted and made his way to the stairs before heading to The Corso. Sam resumed reading the notes and transcripts of the contract. While it could not be proved that Angela committed suicide after the shock of receiving a NOD, Sam couldn't help but feel it was a contributing factor.

"I'm glad that is over" Brianna bemoaned after finishing the call with Jenny. "I can't deal with this, way too many hats to wear in Sensitive Matters. Collections officer, financial counsellor, a therapist-"

"Come on Bree" Sam said, "log out. Let's go to the TAB."

On the floor below on the west side of level 3, Mark Bryers is in a rigid conversation with a credit analyst, Adeel Makhur, over his declining of a car loan application. Adeel, in his early twenties, is in his third year at Global, the entire time of which has been spent as a credit analyst, where he assesses loan applications and makes the decision on whether or not to approve them. He recently graduated from university with a Bachelor of Business Finance, a four-year degree which he achieved whilst also working full-time at Global, no mean feat.

Adeel is a mild-mannered fellow with a gleaming smile and magnetic mien, avails himself to everyone and is well-liked by his colleagues. He is also a stickler for the rules and of the eighteen credit analysts in the Global Car Loans Credit division, he has the highest rate of declined applications. Mark is trying to pressure Adeel into changing his decision and approving it but, as he has always done, Adeel stands his ground.

"The client has already had two loans with us" Mark reasoned, "both of which were paid out."

"They were paid out all right Mark" Adeel agreed, "but the payment history was appalling.

Forty seven dishonoured payments, three times applied for hardship and then there is the credit score."

Inside the TAB Sam and Brianna are sitting at a table in the corner, having ordered only a Win as neither have the stomach to eat anything, preferring a cup of Irish Breakfast tea.

"So you think Ali's actions may have contributed to her suicide?" a stunned Brianna asks. "I didn't think to look at the loan to see what transpired previously."

"Nor did they, hence we can't be hard on Collections" Sam responded "and I'm not saying that Ali's mistakes contributed, there is no way of knowing, but it does bug me a bit. It was purely by chance that when I stopped to have a chinwag with Ali the other day, I casually glanced at the hardship case he was dealing with and observed it was a young girl with a Ford Mustang under finance, which I felt was very unusual. If it hadn't been for those two things I wouldn't have even noticed the account."

"I'm confused," Brianna said, "we did give Angela Rankin hardship assistance or we didn't?"

"A bit of both," Sam replied. "Ali approved the three months of no payments and promised to add the arrears to the end of the loan but failed to code it properly and the hardship assistance was never processed. It resulted in inadvertently being returned to the collections team who didn't notice the error and proceeded to treat it like any other loan in arrears. Next minute they sent a Notice of Demand - and we both know the wording of NODs can be very hard-hitting and to the point - and three days after it was sent, she committed suicide."

Brianna sighed and sipped her tea. She and Sam both sat in silence. To their right was one of the twenty-seven television screens spread throughout the TAB. While the other twenty-six displayed sports and horse racing, this was the only TV to show music, though it was coming to the end of an advertisement for a looming National Rugby League clash between the Manly Sea Eagles and South Sydney Rabbitohs to be held nearby at Brookvale Oval. The advertisement ends and a new song emerges. A car appears with a man driving as the song Everybody Hurts by REM begins to play.

Sam and Brianna gaze at the screen then look at each other as they think of Angela Rankin https://www.youtube.com/watch?v=mhIay4-PbCY

Chapter 13 Financial Abuse

Sam's sleep pattern was taking a bit of a battering, thanks to the growing workload of Sensitive Matters. Normally woken up by the alarm, the last few mornings have seen him awake at least an hour before Everton starts to play. On this particular morning, the alarm isn't due to go off for another fifteen minutes yet Sam is already showered and dressed and making his way to the office.

After disembarking from the Manly ferry, Sam takes his normal route to Global and notices Paddy dining at the TAB so he makes a slight detour and wanders in.

"Top of the morning Paddy" Sam greets, "what are you betting on today?"

"Win and Place Sam" Paddy responds, "helps to keep my eyes clear and voice sharp."

After ordering the same from Carla, Sam joins Paddy at his table, plonking himself on the chair opposite, "I tell you, Paddy" Sam said, "aren't you a sight for sore eyes."

"The day hasn't even started yet Sam" Paddy replied, "and you already look under the pump."

"This new role in Sensitive Matters is much more of a challenge than I thought," Sam explained.

"So how is it so different from your other role?" Paddy asked.

"Well firstly" Sam answered, "we have to cut the BS and bluster, and I especially miss the bluster. Facts only. That takes a lot of reading and researching, understanding all the laws and regulations and with some of these contracts, it's like reading War And Peace. Back in the Late

Arrears days we could pretty much say what we wanted; the key to success was all about being confident and convicted."

"And bully people into paying" Paddy said with a hint of incredulity.

"No Paddy" Sam responded, "it is convincing clients to pay. It's all in the way we say it. For example, I can tell you right now, unequivocally and categorically, that man-made climate change is a crock of the proverbial. Complete and utter nonsense."

"You surely don't believe that, Sam," Paddy rebuked.

"Of course I don't, Paddy" Sam responded, "but for you to even say that shows I had some cut-through. The more confident and convicted you are, the more lies you can tell. It's not the early bird who gets the worm, it is the confident bird who gets the worm. But that's only part of it, it's also the emotional toll it is taking on my team; there is already one member who is showing signs she is on the way to becoming a nervous wreck.'

"So what exactly is Sensitive Matters?" Paddy asked, "it sounds like you deal with government secrets and documents."

"Nah mate" Sam laughed, "this is much more challenging. We look after all the vulnerable clients at Global Car Loans. The people who are victims of domestic violence, financial abuse, suffer mental illness, terminal illnesses, people who pass away deceased estates, you know, people who have had severe misfortune.

"Is the stolen generation on that list?" Paddy asked.

Inside the Global office, Logan is already hard at work. Normally at 7 o'clock on a weekday morning Logan would either be in snoozeville or tackling the Manly surf but on this occasion he is wide awake, at his desk in the office and fully focused on tackling his portfolio.

Meanwhile, after finishing his Win and Place, Paddy left Sam to his own devices and is setting up in the Burrow in preparation for a day of busking. Sam remains at the TAB, devouring a Trifecta as he types on his laptop the plan he discussed the previous day with Bulldog and Stuart. Sam drafts an e-mail, addressed to all other Car Loan departments, with a process document on when it is appropriate to refer a contract to Sensitive Matters and when it is not. He hits send, closes his laptop, bids farewell to Carla and makes a beeline for the office.

When Sam arrives in the Sensitive Matters domain, he is stunned to see Logan at his desk.

"Knock me dead if I'm a jack-in-the-box Logan," Sam blurted, "talk about being up with the sparrows. What happened to 'leave it to the last minute and it only takes a minute?"

"That mindset is on holiday" Logan reacted.

"So, giving the board a rest this morning?" Sam asked

"I see you're not," Logan quipped as he looked at the wallboard behind Sam, filled with facts and figures.

"Yeah well, gotta keep us all informed," Sam explained; these sensitive cases are rising, from 78 on day 1 to 858 now."

"Well I think you need to change the song of the week. And I would never give the board a miss, Sam" Logan continued, "I'm prepared to sacrifice certain things for this job but surfing is not one of them."

"How could you. I would think surfing would be a boon for this job" Sam responded, "any job for that matter, physically and mentally."

"You're not wrong there Sam" Logan agreed, "and when I was out on the waves this morning I couldn't stop thinking of Julia Cranston and Gerassimos Dukas."

"It sounds like you are suffering the same affliction as me, me ol' mate" Sam responded.

"Constantly thinking about sensitive matters and ideas. Your outlet is the ocean, mine is mixing with the Martians."

"Martians?" Logan queries a smiling Sam before returning to explaining why he is early.

"Julia Cranston in particular, has got my goat," Logan explained.

"Yeah" Sam agreed, "she seems to be taking old Gerassimos to the cleaners."

"There is no seems about it Sam" Logan emphasised, "Julia is definitely taking Gerassimos to the cleaners, that is why it's with us under financial abuse. There is so much that simply does not add up. We have provided five hardship assistances, and on every single occasion we have not spoken to the client to script the changes and get the approval, not once. It has all been a signed acceptance."

The conversation was interrupted by Sam's laptop, alerting him to an e-mail he received which was a response to the directive he sent when at the TAB earlier. It was from Ivan Merchant, the Customer Service manager, who was offering to lend some of their team to take calls when it became busy. Sam began typing a response while listening to Logan, thanking him for the offer but rejecting it as he saw it as a band aid solution. Sam also knew from his experience in Collections, who adopted a similar process when they were short-staffed, that it invariably created more work, not less, mainly because the Customer Service agents had a poor understanding of Collections. If it didn't work there it certainly wouldn't work in Sensitive Matters.

"Hey Ivan" Sam wrote, "thanks for the offer, but we'll be fine. As long as your guys can make sure they follow the referral process I outlined; we should be cooking like Betty Crocker. I hope all is well in CS"

"Guess what else I discovered on Friday" Logan continued, "the contract was opened 6 years ago, 112 conversations recorded since then and not once have we spoken to Gerassimos Dukas - it has always been the authorised third party, Julia Cranston."

"Authorised in inverted commas" Sam said. "What, do you think the possibility is that Gerassimos doesn't exist?"

"Ooh" Logan replied, "I never considered that. Surely not."

"He surely not doesn't exist" Sam posed, "or surely not to my suggestion?"

"Have a look at the reasons Julie has given for being unable to pay the loan," Logan replied ignoring Sam's question: "first Gerassimos was hospitalised with liver cancer, on another occasion, his father passed away. Months later Gerassimos' brother was involved in a car accident and not long after that his mother died. There was Covid, of course and the latest reason given is Gerassimos has family in Greece whose home has been impacted by bushfires so he's flown over there to help."

"It's blatantly clear Sam asserted, "this lady is lying through her teeth, can't believe a word she is saying - nought credibility. The problem is, Julie seems to have an answer for everything and while she may not be the client and Gerassimos is solely liable for the debt, due process was followed to indicate he has given full authority for her to act on his behalf, we are pretty much hamstrung."

"I disagree, Sam" Logan reacted, "there has to be something we can do. So I'm out there this morning, at 6 a.m. waiting for a wave, and it occurred to me that there must be a provision for when a third party does not act in the best interests of their client," as he surfed the internet.

"You know what Logan" Sam smiled, "you may be onto something. I suspect ASIC or APRA, maybe even the ombudsman has something to support your notion, unlike King Neptune who didn't have one when the seas dried up."

"Didn't have one what?" Logan quizzed.

"A notion," Sam replied, enunciating it as 'an ocean'.

"I'm trying to be serious, Sam," Logan retorted. "I also think the debt collection guidelines could be the go "as he searched the website and clicked on the Australian Securities and Investments Commission website. "Here we go:

'(d) You are entitled to contact a debtor directly if: the debtor specifically requests direct communication with you the representative does not consent to represent the debtor in relation to the debt the representative advises you that they do not have instructions to represent the debtor in relation to the debt the representative does not respond to your communications within a reasonable time (normally seven days) and you advise the representative in writing after the reasonable time has passed that if they do not respond within the next seven days, you will make direct contact with the debtor you advised the debtor that you require a written authority which states that you are only to communicate through the debtor's representative, and the debtor or representative fails to provide you with that written authority within a reasonable time (normally seven days). Note that this does not apply where the debtor's representative is a solicitor. When an authorised representative does not agree to have written correspondence redirected to them, such correspondence should continue to be sent directly to the debtor.'

An intrigued Sam also brought up the Debt Collection Guidelines on his laptop, a website he already had in his favourites directory.

"It also says" Sam interjected, "You may also be entitled to contact a debtor directly where more than one of the following (except where the representative is a financial counsellor, a qualified legal practitioner in the relevant state or territory, or a qualified accountant): the representative is acting in a manner or making decisions which increase or are likely to increase the debtor's liabilities.

"Brilliant" Logan beamed, "Come nine o'clock. I am going to ring Julie, find out Gerassimos'

phone number in Greece and propose to ring him myself. I don't care about the time difference."

Out of the blue, Griggsy made an appearance and placed a letter on Sam's desk.

"This is your domain now Sam," Griggsy says before heading towards the kitchen, keen to raid the Tim Tam jar. Sam picks up the letter to find it is from a federal member of Parliament, Parliament, Claire Neale addressed to Global's CEO. It's dated two weeks ago, making Sam think it took that long for someone to work out who should address it.

Claire is polite but candid. She writes that she has been dealing with a Global client, Melissa Carson, who is a victim of severe family violence and is being supported by three different charities.

The family violence was perpetrated against Ms Carson over a long term and she now owes tens of thousands of dollars as a consequence of the abusive relationship. This stemmed from being forced to borrow and take out loans, through threats of and actual violence by the perpetrator. Fortunately Ms Carson is out of the violent situation and is trying to get back on her feet.

Towards the end of the letter Sam learns of the primary reason for the missive: the MP is seeking a debt waiver. The penultimate paragraph is telling: "It is very clear to me that the community expects the financial services industry to understand and appreciate the impacts of family violence and appropriately manage debts incurred in this context."

It's not uncommon for a client or representative to seek a debt waiver. Often it will be a not-for-profit financial counsellor acting on behalf of the client who lacks the knowledge or strength to pursue this on their own. But never, to Sam's knowledge, has the request come from a federal politician.

Sam picks up the letter and, rises from his chair and walks to the stairs before heading out of the building thinking a Win, and the Irish Breakfast tea on the TAB's menu, will be just what the doctor ordered. As he approaches the cafe, Sam notices Brianna striding down The Corso heading for the office, only for her to see Sam and makes a detour in his direction.

"I'm intrigued to know about this meeting you booked for 8.30," Brianna said. "What is VEW?"

"Win, Place or Daily Double?" Sam asked Brianna as she joined him walking to the TAB.

Over in The Burrow, it's virtually standing room only for the buskers after Paddy, who is sitting behind his keyboard, has been joined by Ronnie as they prepare to perform the day's first song together. The Corso is swarming with shoppers, tourists, and people making their way to work, with many having stopped to get some uplift from Manly's favourite buskers.

Ronnie is on electric guitar while Paddy prepares to be the lead vocalist for their rendition of Silverchair's "Straight Lines".

Silverchair - Straight Lines w/ Lyrics

Chapter 14 Vew Golf

In what seems the twinkling of an eye, the morning turns into the afternoon as Sam pushes his whiteboard on wheels along the fourth-floor west hallway. He arrives at meeting room 4.11, where Mary and Logan are seated, each in their own world, reading material on their respective laptops. As Sam pushes towards the back of the room, Mary looks up to see a very different whiteboard to the one filled with statistics and KPIs the team had witnessed on a daily basis. In bold lettering is "VEW GOLF - Verbal, Electronic, Written "Darn" Logan sighed, "The Bills got done."

"I thought you looked more upbeat and sprightly today Logan," Sam greeted as he and Brianna walked into the room. "I gather you weren't up at 3 in the morning watching the gridiron, or should I say American Football."

"That's why you are on the big bucks," Logan sarcastically responded.

"He's also, as am I" Mary interjected, "keen to know what this VEW Golf is all about, though the whiteboard gives us some idea."

"VEW Golf" "Sam responded as he walked to the whiteboard, "is something I dreamed up whilst in the shower. It's our model on how we deal with Sensitive clients. I reviewed some of our KPIs and our contact rate has been steadily dropping. Granted, we are tackling the contracts more quickly now, which is good, but they are dragging out because we aren't making the contact we once were."

"It's no different to Late Arrears Sam" Logan interjected, "the clients are not answering the Phone," as Brianna walks in the door.

"Good morning, everyone" Brianna greeted, "I hope you didn't start this meeting without me."

"Hey Bree" Sam reacted, "not at all, in fact, your timing is perfect. I was just explaining that our contact rate has dropped, meaning we are taking longer to resolve each contract and the reason, which relates to your point Logan, is we aren't telephoning clients anywhere near as much. Our main means of communicating now is e-mail."

Brianna sat down next to Mary and placed her laptop on the desk leaving it closed as she listened to Sam.

"When Sensitive Matters kicked off, we were speaking to a lot of the clients on the phone, and engineering a resolution on that call - one interaction. But over time the phone calls have dropped markedly and been replaced by e-mail, which have soared but taking six or seven interactions to engineer a resolution. Hence why I thought of VEW. From now on, I want every form of correspondence with clients to be tackled in this order. Our first attempt is always on the phone - verbal. If that fails, the next effort will be via e-mail - electronic. And if both of these are unsuccessful, then send a letter via post – written."

"I'm already doing that Sam" Logan reacted, "I'm a step ahead of you. I just didn't look at it as VEW, that's all."

"I know you are Logan" Sam replied, "hats off to you, and your results speak for themselves; this is about the whole team adopting a similar approach."

"I prefer e-mail Sam" Brianna advised, "it's less confronting."

"It's also less efficient Bree" Sam stressed "and one of the reasons we aren't keeping up with the workload. We get them on the phone, discuss the pros and cons and resolve the matter then and there. First contact resolution. With e-mail we are taking an inordinate amount of time to deal with what often are relatively basic issues. So many missives back and forth, it has turned into e-mail ping pong."

"Makes sense," Mary remarked, "I prefer to talk to the clients anyway."

"Last month" Sam added, "we resolved 57 sensitive matters - 46 of them were after we spoke to the client on the phone. Of the 11 others, the total time spent working these accounts was more than the 46 we did over the phone - it's a no-brainer."

On the other side of the Sydney, in their home in Turramurra, Vincent is dressed and ready for school, with his satchel on his back and carrying a gym bag.

"Looks like you are all set and ready for the big day, Vincent" Abbey enthused.

"Is Dad still coming, Mum?" Vincent asked.

"He said he would," Abbey replied as she opened the door to leave for school. "He wants to see you in your debut dramatical performance and break a leg."

Sam promised to attend Vincent's first school play, which was scheduled for 3 o'clock in the afternoon, and whilst Abbey expressed confidence to Vincent he would be there, deep down Sam's history of unreliability made her slightly dubious.

Back at Global, Sam is impressing upon the team the merits of VEW Golf.

"We also can't be too sure about who is responding to an e-mail either," Sam reasoned. The financial abuse case is a good example."

"OK" Mary interjected, "that is pretty straightforward. But what does this have to do with golf.

Are you organising some sort of golf day?"

"Not golf day Mary" Sam responded, "golf week."

Sam starts writing on the whiteboard:

Day 1,

Day 2

Moving Day

"In professional golf," Sam explains, "there are four rounds played over 4 days, and Days 1 and 2 are mainly about making the cut."

"What's the cut?" Mary asked.

"The cut" Sam explained "is where the field of say 120 pro golfers is cut to around 60. This means the top 60 get to play the remaining two rounds while the bottom sixty are eliminated, or cut. So on those first two days you don't want to do anything rash or risky and put yourself out of contention.

And all the while you have an eye on the leaderboard. In our case, the leaderboard is the alpha split, or each of your portfolios. I want you to compete against each other to bring down your portfolios which, at the same time, will reduce the arrears index."

"You're not planning to sack any of us, are you Sam?" Brianna asked.

"What!" Sam responded incredulously, "you couldn't be further from the truth, there will be no 'cut' here but I do want you to focus on putting your portfolios in the prime position for Moving Day, which for us will be Wednesdays and Thursdays. They are the days where all your preparation of the previous two days will lead to people either paying their arrears or relinquishing the vehicle."

Sam receives a message from Johnny Kep and pauses to read it. "The Mustang is in stock, mate, what do you want to do with it?"

"I have to go," Sam continues, "I have to see Johnny Kep but, as with everything, if anything lacks clarity or you're unsure just give me a bugle."

Sam leaves the room and heads across the floor to Johnny's desk. Along the way he passes through his old team of Late Arrears, many of whom are on calls with clients so he gives his former collections colleagues a wave, careful to not interrupt them. He knows they are under pressure, having been given a directive from Bulldog to go harder on tardy payers due to the poor state of the arrears index. On one of the calls, Roy Benz is in a heated discussion with a customer.

"I'll tell you for the last time" Roy stresses, "you either pay the arrears by 5 p.m. today or expect to see the mercantile agent again rock up to your house again but this time it will be different.

He won't come there with a demand to pay the arrears, he will come there with a tow truck to take away the car. You will then have to cover all of the agent's costs......."

"Check out my watch, Sam?" Johnny offered as Sam arrived at his desk.

Sam looked at Johnny's wrist and saw a watch with the time set in spaces of ten minutes, as opposed to the standard five.

"I don't get it" Sam reacted.

"What idiot," Johnny explained, "came up with the concept of having a clock or watch with 5 minute intervals but not telling you the time?" Sam looked even more puzzled.

"On my watch" Johnny added, "you don't need to times the number by 5 - such as the quarter hour being a 3 so you multiply it by 5, and you get 15 minutes past the hour. I mean holy gravioli, what a headache. Now you just go: 1 equals 10, 2 equals 20, 3 equals 30 and so on. One less way for the government to control me"

"The Mustang," Sam said, "what sort of condition is it in and have you had a chance to value it?"

"Top condition, Sam" Johnny responded, "and yes, we are looking at around $55,000 - $58,000.

"Wow," Sam exclaimed, that's more than what is owed on the loan."

Sam realised that if the vehicle sold for the amount Johnny indicated, this would leave a surplus in excess of $15,000. Normally when this happens the bank is obliged to pay the extra funds to the client but in this case, Sam thought, there is no living client. Sam also knew Gavin loved it when a sale at auction produced surplus funds as his unwritten policy was that unless the client specifically asks for it, the surplus funds stay with the bank. Good for the arrears index and their monthly bonuses.

Meanwhile, Roy has ended his heated call. Often referred to as Mr Post Mortem, for his love of discussing robust calls with his teammates, Roy is revelling in sharing with Sean his latest clash.

"6 weeks of messages, e-mail, calls and not a peep from the debtor. Now he rings." Roy barked "The benefits of mercantile agents." Sean observed.

"That's when cash or keys becomes a reality" Roy said cheerily. "Of course, he thought he could just lie through his teeth, tried to tell me he'd never broken an arrangement with us, but when I recapped the history with the exact dates and times of the conversations where he agreed to pay, he changed his tune."

"It's always good when you can provide facts and figures to counter their argument," Sean said concurringly.

"We have the upper hand" Roy enthused, "I love it when I prove that the debtor is wrong. And the thing they seem to forget is that it is entirely their fault. I wouldn't be chasing these recalcitrants if they did what they pledged to do when they signed the contract, and paid the bloody loan."

"It's a good thing they don't," Sean said, "otherwise we'd be out of a job."

"We will always have a job," Roy said smugly, "because there will always be deadbeat Debtors."

Out in the Burrow, Sherese is coming to the end of a solo performance and from a distance, Paddy approaches. Sherese addresses the large gathering who have enjoyed her trumpet solos.

"And for my final tune today" Sherese boomed, "I want to pay tribute to one of my favourite

Aussie artists, Johnny Farnham."

Paddy then jumped into the Burrow and began playing the keyboard before Sherese started singing Johnny Farnham's version of the Beatles hit "Help."

https://www.youtube.com/watch?v=IoMcR_T5M1g

Chapter 15 Deceased Estate

"What is a grant of probate?" Logan shouts from his desk, as he reads an e-mail concerning a client who passed away.

Logan, Mary, and Brianna are at their desks in the Sensitive Matters domain tackling their respective portfolios. The broad scope afforded to their unit has meant a wide range of topics and material emerging every day, often for the first time. Logan's understanding of complex matters has improved markedly over recent weeks, but, like his colleagues, he continues to come across accounts which present posers and terms of which he has never heard. Today is no exception.

'Look it up Logan" Brianna sneered while muting her phone during a conversation with a client:

"A grant of probate," Mary interjects, is a legal document that authorises an executor named in the will to manage the estate of a deceased person in accordance with the provisions of the deceased's will.

"Oh great, thanks Mary" Logan replies enthusiastically, "I have a case here where the client passed away but the wife, who is not on the contract, wants to keep the car.

She says she will pay out the loan after a grant of probate."

"That's a good sign, Logan" Mary responded, "at least that suggests the client left a will, something many people don't."

"Well," Logan posed, becoming more intrigued, "the e-mail doesn't actually say the client left a will. What if there isn't one?"

"Then someone will need to apply for a Letter of Administration" Mary responded, "which is a legal document issued by the court which allows the administrator to manage and distribute the deceased's assets. This can be issued when there is no named executor in the will that is willing to administer the will OR if there is no will. But in this case, the fact she is applying for probate suggests there is a will."

Logan nods appreciatively and returns to reviewing the account which now falls into the category of Deceased Estates. Brianna continues her conversation on the phone with the client while Mary, ever conscious of the inbound call queue, which currently has none, prepares to ring a customer from her portfolio when she is approached by a team member from Customer

Service, Emily, a shy, softly spoken, bespectacled middle-aged lady with long curly hair who appears flustered.

When the Sensitive Matters team was formed, they were allocated desks on a different floor to the rest of Arrears Management. While there are no set seating allocations, designed for what is described as a "hot-desk environment", Sam observed that Mary, Logan, and Brianna either unintentionally or by design sat at the same desk each day, a habit of which he was not fond. He also didn't like being isolated from the rest of their colleagues so gained approval from Gavin to move back to the floor where they were based, arguing it will give his team the opportunity to engage and share their knowledge of vulnerable clients, helping them to deal with them. This meant that Collections and Customer Service sat within a hop, skip, and a jump of his team.

"Sorry to bother you Mary" Emily says "but I have a client on the line who is threatening to kill himself."

Mary promptly stops dialling and rises from her chair, concerned for Emily, who is visibly shaken.

"Are you OK, Emily?" Mary asked.

"I'm all right, Mary" Emily replied, "I'm just glad there was someone here to deal with this type of call, I couldn't imagine what I'd do if you guys weren't here."

Sam walks in after his time with Johnny Kep and notices Emily talking to Mary.

"Is everything OK ladies?" Sam asks.

"Emily has a tough call" Mary responded, "so I am just going to her desk to speak to the client."

Sam nods as they walk off together, Mary with an arm around Emily's shoulder. Normally a call would be transferred and Mary could take it in the more comfortable surrounds of her desk, computer and colleagues but Sam sensed this was very serious and backed Mary's judgement.

Before Sam had a chance to sit at his desk, Brianna approached, looking disquieted, "I need to take next week off Sam; something has come up."

"Are you all right?" Sam asked

"I think so," Brianna replied before a long pause. "Have you got a minute?"

"Of course," Sam responded reassuringly, "let's find a meeting room."

"When you get back, Sam" a slightly flustered Logan interrupted, "I need you to take a look at this vulnerable client," as he stood before Sam and Brianna armed with his laptop and revealing the details of Gemma Campbell's account."

"I took a call from Gemma yesterday at about 4.45 and finished speaking to her about an hour later" Logan added, "she is in dire straits."

"Give me half-an-hour or so Logan" Sam said, "when I get back, it will be my top priority."

As Sam and Brianna went scouting for a spare meeting room, they walked past the Skybox where Mark Bryers, Gavin, Stu, Eric and Sean are seated around the table, all looking at the giant screen at the front revealing Renita speaking to them via Zoom. Sam knows what the meeting is about and had he been in his former role in Collections, would've also been in attendance where the discussion revolves around a recent audit undertaken with dealerships financed by Global.

As part of Global's involvement with the car loan industry, it finances over 100 dealerships around Australia, worth around $400million. Essentially, every vehicle that is on the car lot at one of these dealerships is financed by Global. Included in the contractual agreement is that when a dealership sells a car via finance, Global must be given the first right of refusal. Concerns had been raised by Renita that this wasn't broadly happening and instructed Gavin to send two people on a mission to audit the dealerships in question. After three weeks Eric and Sean determined these fears were well founded. They also discovered, after conducting a stocktake, that there were vehicles missing with no record of them ever being sold.

"I was never a fan of outlaying over $400million to these dealerships in the first place" Renita opined, "and what you have uncovered Gavin reinforces my view."

"It's not as bad as it looks, Renita" Mark reacted, "these dealerships didn't know we were coming and just hadn't updated their records."

Mark is a staunch supporter of the dealerships as they not only bring Global a lot of sales, they also boost their commissions through the range of insurances they sell to unwitting clients. Though Global has a sales division where potential clients can apply directly for a loan, the vast majority of business, about 90%, is done with intermediaries such as car dealerships and finance brokers, and as far as Mark is concerned, they come first.

"Of course they didn't know we were coming, Mark," Renita reacted, "that is the whole point.

We weren't about to give them time to doctor their books."

Sam and Brianna have found an empty room, 4.11. When inside Sam pulled out a chair for Brianna, who slowly sat down and whose look of disquiet is now turned to a look of being on the verge of tears.

My closest friend has been rushed to hospital, and I need to visit him," Brianna explained.

"That's terrible, Bree" Sam responded. "Sorry to hear that. Sure, take next week off; just submit the leave request today if you can."

"Actually, can we make it two?" Brianna answered.

"Two, as in two weeks?" a slightly befuddled Sam asked

"My friend lives in New Zealand," Brianna explained.

Sam sat silently, thinking primarily not of Bree's wellbeing but of the rising number of vulnerable clients in her portfolio and the extra pressure it would place on his already overworked team. Brianna was the primary cause to introduce VEW as she was the main culprit for e-mailing and not ringing clients. On the flip side, he could utilise the two weeks by splitting her portfolio between Mary and Logan and compare their results to Brianna's.

"Two weeks it is Bree," Sam responds, "I hope your friend gets better."

As they both get up from the desk, Sam receives a text message; it's from Abbey: "where are you!!!!!!!"

"Damn" Sam bemoaned, remembering he was supposed to attend Vincent's drama which starts at 3.00. His watch read 3.05.

Vincent is on stage for the school play and has the lead role. Abbey is seated in the packed crowd with every seat taken, except for one - the seat next to Abbey.

Sam was experiencing something new: the thought of missing an occasion to do with Vincent was slightly disconcerting. As he pondered, Logan bailed him up, keen to revisit the case he mentioned before Sam and Brianna left for their meeting. "Hey Sam, Gemma Campbell, yesterday's 4.45 call" Logan pressed.

"So what time did you get home?" Sam asked, quickly diverting his focus to Logan, aware he would've walked out of the office no less than an hour past his scheduled finishing time.

"It wasn't too bad," Logan answered, "I missed a yoga session but so be it" to which Sam nodded appreciatively.

"I need you to waive her debt," Logan asserted, "$6K. Gemma lost everything, including her house, in the bushfires."

"Sounds like you are taking a leaf out of Mary's book," Sam said.

"Mary's been an inspiration," Logan replied, "when it comes to helping the vulnerable clients,

she is like a dog with a bone."

"I take it the car is a write-off?" Sam posed.

The funny thing is" Logan said, "if you can have something which is funny in this tragic situation, it is that Gemma still has the car. Completely intact, not a scratch or a burn mark on it. Mary might even call this a GLAM for Gemma, getting this loan, that is, because she literally lost everything, home, pets, furniture .... Thank God we financed the car because that is her home right now."

Sam sighed and again thought of Vincent. "Mate, just e-mail me the details and I'll have a look at it."

"What" a surprised Logan responded, "so there is a chance you will waive it?"

Sam shrugged his shoulders giving a hint of a possible maybe, and peered at the large television screen above which has been commandeered by Mary for the afternoon. After tiring of watching promos and boasts about Global, Mary convinced Sam of the merits in having music videos play for part of the time, and it was agreed she could put YouTube on two afternoons per week and today was one of those occasions.

An unfamiliar group, featuring a lead singer, a guitarist, and a keyboardist, appeared playing outside what looked to be a swimming pool in which women performed synchronised swimming. Sam was taken by the intro, beat, and lyrics, and for the next three minutes, he sat watching Eskimo Joe performing- "FROM THE SEA"

https://www.youtube.com/watch?v=KzAUyjmedCA

Chapter 16 The Removalist

The following morning, on the last day of the working week, Sam arrived at the Sensitive Matters domain to find Logan was already at his desk. In the Late Arrears days this would've brought a flippant remark from colleagues, shocked he would be the first to arrive but in Sensitive Matters early starts were becoming frequent and something Sam unwittingly accepted as the norm.

"Gee whiz, it is hard to get a park around here," Sam bemoaned, "The closest I could get was five streets away."

"You drove in today?" Logan asked, "ferries not working?"

"I have to leave a bit early as I have something on," Sam answered.

The previous day's events irked Sam. The mounting sensitive cases, Bree wanting two weeks off and forgetting Vincent's school play. While there was little he could do - for now - about the first two, there was something he could do about the third matter. Sam felt the need to speak to Vincent and Abbey in person, so drove into work with the idea of finishing early so he can visit them at after-school pick-up.

Make sure you check in on Mary will you Sam?" Logan implored, "she had a real tough call yesterday, suicide."

"The client with Emily" Sam suggested

"Nothing happened in the end," Logan added

"I'm told Mary handled it brilliantly but when you have a guy on the other end of the line threatening to kill himself, I can only imagine it can take its toll. Fortunately, I have never experienced one myself and pray I never will."

Sam didn't say a word. He dropped his bag on his desk and dialled Mary's number, there was no answer.

"It's probably a good time to raise this Sam" Logan said, "I think we should be given some professional training on how to deal with some of these vulnerable clients. This is way harder than I or any of the team imagined."

"You are" Sam replied, "and thanks for mentioning it, great point" as Mary walked in the door.

"Hey Mary" Sam greeted, "great to see you, let's go to the TAB. Logan, hold my calls," he added jestingly.

Logan rued the lost opportunity. He had intended to raise the Sandie Chan matter, where the client sought to be removed from the loan. He also took Mary's advice and delved deeper to see what he could find out for himself and discovered the Banking Code Of Practice (BCOP) did have a section covering this, which seemed to support Sandie's stance, chapter 17 # 56, "You may end your liability by giving us a written request to do so in the following circumstances: Where credit has not been provided or relied upon". In Sandie's case, she signed up to a loan for a Ford Ranger, 4-wheel drive, which was used by her, now, ex-partner, for his construction business. Logan was fairly confident there were grounds to remove Sandie from the loan, especially as it turned out she didn't have a driver's license and didn't know how to drive. Logan watched Sam and Mary head to the TAB, thinking that whilst on the one hand he was disappointed he didn't speak to Sam about it, he felt pleased with himself that he did, this time, "look it up Logan". He was also more concerned for Mary's wellbeing and knew his matter could wait.

As Sam and Mary head towards the stairs they pass the Skybox in which Gavin, Stuart, and Eric are sitting, all in apparent deep discussion. Gavin notices Sam, jumps to his feet, and opens the door.

"Hey Sam" "once you finish whatever you are doing I need you in here."

Sam looks a little concerned, which is noticed by Mary. "I'll be fine Sam" Mary said, "you go and we can catch up at the TAB later."

Mary smiles and heads back to her desk while Sam walks in to join the others.

"Is everything OK with her?" Gavin asked.

"She'll be all right, Bulldog" Sam replied, "what's on the agenda?"

"Don't guess, repossess," Eric answered, "Bulldog's new saying for Collections."

"If you have any doubt, if you are umming and ahhing" Gavin stressed, "err on the side of caution."

"So in those instances," Sam sought to clarify, "you don't want to repossess."

"No!" Gavin thundered, "just the opposite. If you have any doubt, err on the side of caution and repossess. Because if there is some doubt it means there must also be some merit in repossessing."

"Does this apply to Sensitive Matters?" Sam asked.

"It applies to everyone," Gavin replied, "and there are a lot of contracts in Sensitive which fall into this category."

Over in Asset Disposal, Johnny is preparing for the upcoming Luxury Car Auction to be held by Pymbles. Repossessed vehicles from around the country are entered for this six-monthly event which attracts many high-end and well-heeled buyers. Pymbles provides a "Pre-Auction Report"

which reveals Global has 11 vehicles listed for this auction and if the valuations are realised, will nett close to $800,00. Johnny has double-checked the valuations and reserves placed and is now onto the final part of the preparation: informing Pymbles of the names of the Global representatives who will attend.

Gavin and Stuart frequent every auction, luxury and general, mainly because of the free food and alcohol on offer. Johnny is a teetotaller but must be there in a work capacity, including the task of entering into negotiations with prospective purchasers in the event the reserve is not met. On this occasion Johnny adds a new name to the list of Global representatives: Sam Crews.

Back in the skybox, Gavin receives a phone call "Mr Scholes, I presume," Gavin answered, "are you downstairs? (pause) "I'll be right down.

(rises from his chair) John Scholes is here, fellas, I'll be right back."

Though Sam had never met John Scholes, he knew who he was: the owner of Global's number one repossession agent, Scholes Mercantile.

Moments later Gavin returns with John Scholes, who has met Stuart but not Eric or Sam and to whom Gavin introduces accordingly. John, short, corpulent and bald, and in his late sixties, has been involved in the mercantile agency profession for almost fifty years, starting as a collections officer at a regional bank before working his way up the management chain until branching out on his own to form Scholes Mercantile.

He also holds a Commercial Agents and Private Inquiry (CAPI) license.

"Fellas," Gavin said, "John is the guru of collections and mercantile agents. You could write a book about what he doesn't know in the industry but fill a library of what he does know. Now lads"

Gavin says enthusiastically, "let's talk repossessions."

Outside the office, on The Corso, two young males, each dressed in a tuxedo are in The Burrow, performing A capella, singing the Pentatonix song "A Light In The Room" in The Burrow.

https://www.youtube.com/watch?v=sp7PS_UN8Lo

Behind them, about two metres back, Paddy and Sherese Murray are preparing to set up the instruments and stands for the day's play. Like her cousin, Sherese is proficient in multiple instruments with a powerful contralto singing voice. Paddy looks up to see Ronnie making his way to join them. It's an unusual sight for Paddy, to see Ronnie without his beloved Akubra.

"Me ol china," Paddy greets, "where's your hat? I can't remember seeing you without it"

"Why would you want to wear a hat when you have such great hair?" Sherese quipped.

Ronnie smiled. "This must be the delightful and charming cousin you've been telling me about Paddy" Ronnie reacted.

"And this must be the me ol china you've been telling me about," Sherese responded as they both hugged. Sherese hails from Alice Springs and was attempting to forge a career in music but wasn't making the progress for which she had hoped. On a visit by Paddy to see his family in Far North Queensland, he caught up with Sherese and encouraged her to join him in Manly. That was eighteen months ago. Sherese has some similar characteristics to Paddy but impulsiveness isn't one of them. While she liked Paddy's suggestion she would only act on it when she was good and ready. A year and a half later, she kissed her family and friends goodbye, loaded up her Kombi van, and spent the next three days driving to Manly.

"So what's with the monkey suits?" Ronnie asks Paddy while glancing at the chaps singing in front of them.

"These guys are from the Con, better known as the Sydney Conservatorium of Music" Paddy explained, "a couple of tenors, Jeff and Hampton. I decided to reintroduce one day each week where busking is open season, anyone who wants to have a go can perform from the Burrow and hopefully gain greater exposure, not to mention earn a few bucks in the process. That was how the Burrow began and operated for many months until a few of the punters suggested we stick with certain performers each day so they knew who was on when. But I've always loved the open season mindset so I posted something on our social media pages, and these guys are the first cab off the rank."

As planned, Sam left work at 1.30 that afternoon and made the hour-long drive to Turramurra to see Abbey and Vincent after school, which was due to finish at 3.00. He knew Abbey would arrive at around 2.50 p.m. and didn't want to be noticed so he parked three streets away waiting for school to finish. His timing was exquisite. Just as he turned the corner, out of the school's main entrance emerged Abbey and Vincent, among the throng of other parents and children in a similar boat. Sam beeped his horn and drove alongside, beckoning them both to get in the car. An excited Vincent jumped in the back without hesitation, while Abbey was more circumspect, waiting a few seconds before getting into the front passenger's seat. Vincent leans over and he and Sam make the best of a hug in the cramped confines.

"I'm really sorry I missed your school play Vince" Sam began, "this new role of mine is swamping me."

Abbey wanted to castigate Sam but was conscious Vincent was in the car and the effect it would have on him. Abbey wasn't sure if Sam included Vincent deliberately, to avoid her wrath, or if he genuinely was sorry but her instincts told her it was the latter.

"You missed a great show" Abbey replied, "and our Vincent was the star."

They continued to chat as Sam also puts a song on his player "You know I was lying in bed last night listening to ABC Classical and this came on." Sam revealed. Pachelbel's Canon in D Minor promulgated from the radio.

"Remember this?' Sam probed.

"Our one-year anniversary," Abbey smiled, "how could I forget, one of the best nights of my Life."

"Though I almost did," Sam admitted as he turned around and looked at his son, "forget. You know Vince,

I'd planned to book a restaurant and a violinist only to completely forget, making me scurry around for someone at the last minute."

'Well you know what they say Sam" Abbey smiled, "leave it to the last minute, and it only takes a minute."

"Was he good?" Vincent asked innocently.

"It wasn't a he" Abbey replied smilingly. "It was a them."

"Yes son" Sam added, "there were four of them, called themselves the Four Fiddlers. It was quite uncanny actually because I spent an aeon at work searching for a violinist on the internet, to no avail, and then when I left the office I walked out into The Manly Corso, and there they were, playing in the Burrow."

"What's The Burrow?" Vincent asked.

Sam looked at Abbey as it dawned on him he had never introduced his son to his cherished Burrow and good friend Paddy. For that matter, he had never taken him to Manly.

"Well, son," Sam responded, "the only way for me to answer your inspired question is to take you there and you can find out for yourself."

The tension shown by Abbey had now gone, and they talked about the school show with a chirpy Vincent dominating the conversation. All the while Pachelbel's Canon in D Minor continued to play.

https://www.youtube.com/watch?v=9nX_ReyaetE

Chapter 17 Mental Illness

"This mental illness as a reason for not paying is getting out of hand, Stu" Gavin whined as he polished off another schooner at their favourite meeting room, The Staines Hotel. "We have nine categories under Sensitive Matters: Deceased, financial abuse, mental illness, domestic violence, terminal illness (which generously includes a family member), natural disaster, homelessness, threats of self-harm and elder abuse. Do you know what percentage of the entire book is coded to mental illness?"

"Umm" Stuart shrugged, "aroun-"Fifty-eight!" Gavin thundered, not enabling Stuart the opportunity to answer. "That means three out of every five accounts in the Sensitive Matters portfolio are due to mental illness. This is Australia for crying out loud, God's country, the land of opportunity, how can you get depressed here.

People are taking the piss" as Eric joins them, clasping three schooners of Carlton Dry.

"The trouble is Bulldog," Stuart responded, "the mental illness is the reason they stop working and if they're not working, they don't have an income so can't pay the loan."

"Well no Stu" Bulldog countered, "plenty of them are working. I was looking at one account, where the debtor has engaged one of those financial counsellors who has claimed mental illness because the debtor is a gambler. How is gambling a mental illness? People punt because they like it, they love the thrill of a win. When they win it's a mental euphoria. When they lose it's a mental illness."

"So you reckon we should be ramping up repossessions for these mental illness cases" Stuart posed.

"Absolutely" Bulldog responded, "and we'd be doing them - and others - a huge favour. The trouble with mental illness is that the people who suffer it, just don't care - about other people. Of course they care about themselves; that is all they care about, but their loved ones, those who suffer through no fault of their own, they couldn't give a hoot about them. It shouldn't be called mental illness, it should be called selfish illness, Eric and Stuart remained tight-lipped, both disagreeing with Bulldog's analysis but not game to challenge him.

'Something needs to be done about these sensitive cases where they simply stop paying,"

Gavin continued, "that was never my purpose of this team and it's killing the arrears index" he stressed.

It occurred to Stuart that the Sensitive Matters team was Renita's concept but he stayed silent.

"Some of the Sensitive accounts haven't had a payment in 12 months or more" Eric conveyed.

Back in the office, with Sam leaving early, the Sensitive team is down to Brianna, Logan and Mary.

While Brianna spent three years as a team leader, Sam opted to ask Mary to look after the SM crew while he was away and if anything happens which she struggles to handle, to give him a bugle. Sam wasn't sidelining Brianna, rather giving Mary an opportunity after she expressed a desire to become a team leader in her career development discussions. Mary kept one keen eye on the inbound calls queue and the other on her team and noticed Brianna on the phone - her personal mobile - visibly distressed.

Logan, who was on the company phone to a vulnerable client, also noticed his upset colleague. Mary rose from her desk and slowly approached . The call ended with Brianna in tears.

Before Mary could say anything, Brianna rose from her desk, "I just need a few minutes," she uttered, avoiding eye contact, "that was a call from the mental facility" as she headed to the bathroom.

Mary stood there in silence, unsure whether she should follow Brianna or ring Sam. She opted for the former.

Mary gingerly entered the bathroom to find Brianna sobbing uncontrollably. She instinctively put arms around her and they hugged.

"It's my friend," Brianna sobbed, "the one I'm flying to New Zealand to see. He passed away today."

It was now five o'clock meaning the Sensitive Matters lines had just closed. Logan's call with the vulnerable client ended but he was more worried about his vulnerable colleague. He sat wondering what to do before muttering to himself, "I have to know she is OK" as he tossed his headphones on his desk and headed to the bathroom. Seemingly unconcerned it was the women's toilets, he knocked on the main door and walked in to find Brianna and Mary still embracing. "I was worried about you Bree."

Brianna didn't respond while Mary motioned to Logan to leave, indicating not to worry and she will look after her. "I'm off to the TAB," Logan said as he was leaving, subtly suggesting they could join him there.

Outside, in The Corso, a number of shops are closing up for the day. Like many of its restaurant and cafe counterparts, the TAB and will remain open until 11 p.m. Inside, there is a scattering of diners with about half of the tables empty but from 6 o'clock, they are fully booked. As Carla tucks some chairs into the tables, she sees Logan in the distance, sprinting towards her. "Any chance we can have three Daily Doubles and a table Carla?" Logan asks. "I know you get booked out around this time."

"There is always a table for you Logan" Carla says, smiling.

"You are a legend" Logan said as Carla noticed Mary and Brianna approaching from a distance. As they get closer Carla observes Mary's arm around Brianna's shoulder and the solemn look on each of their faces and realises something serious has happened. "Take your favourite table, over there under the YouTube TV. Take as long as you want." Carla said reassuringly.

Once seated, a more composed Brianna shared the reasons for her reaction with Logan and Mary.

"He was my best friend, known him since I was five years old and though he lives in New Zealand, we stay in touch all the time, we see each other at least four times a year," Brianna explained.

"I was initially told he had mental health problems and, so, was admitted to a facility but I wasn't told he was suicidal. As I later found out, it wasn't a mental health facility to where he was admitted but a hospital after his suicide attempt, from which he didn't recover."

Carla arrives with the first leg of their Daily Doubles, placing a cup of English Breakfast tea in front of Brianna, Mary and Logan.

"Tea leaves in a pot" Carla said, "just how you like it, Brianna."

Brianna smiled, her first for some time. "Second leg of the Daily Double is on its way," Carla added before heading back to the kitchen. The mood was starting to lighten and Mary felt relieved they were on the doorstep of the weekend, allowing Brianna to have some time away from Sensitive Matters.

The following Monday morning Sam, as per the norm, is in the office well before his team arrives. It's 7.15 and Sam has his eyes firmly fixed on his computer, of a photo of Abbey, Vincent and him when they were one. Mary decided not to inform Sam of Bree's experience, preferring to tell him in person. Bree arrives early and approaches the Sensitive area from behind Sam, catching a glimpse of the photo.

"Good morning, Sam" Brianna said, "that's a nice photo, who is it of?"

Sam quickly closes his laptop, fiercely averse to any of his team knowing about his private life.

"Wow" Sam remarked and ignoring Brianna's question, "aren't you an early bird."

"I came in early because I need to talk to you, Sam" Brianna explained, "do you have a minute or two?"

All of the meeting rooms are empty leaving Sam a swag of choices as he opts for 4.43. As they sit down, Brianna wastes no time in explaining her early arrival. After revealing the previous afternoon's chain of events, Brianna expands to the SM role.

"I am really struggling to cope, Sam" Brianna laments. "Even without what happened in NZ, I've been having a hard time with it. Mental illness, domestic violence, homelessness, terminal illnesses, cancer, deceased, it's just relentless, every call, there's no respite. I'm expected to be a collections officer, a financial counsellor, a therapist."

"But didn't you have these sort of cases in Hardship?" Sam reasoned.

"Yes" Brianna responded, "but they were the exception. Most people wanted hardship assistance after losing their job, unemployment. Plus I rarely spoke to a client, I was the team leader remember. And in Hardship we could offer a solution. The assistance we provided was always for the short term but in Sensitive Matters it's either long-term or infinity. And quite frankly, most of the time we simply do not have a solution," as Sam nodded understandingly.

"And this VEW model" Brianna continued, "with your insistence on us following it verbatim, is just making it worse for me." Sam sat stone-faced, unsure of how to react. He was convinced VEW was the perfect process to adopt, believing his team would see it similarly. Tinkering with the format was not an option to Sam but he sensed Brianna was about to ask for it to be watered down and speak to less customers. Brianna had other ideas.

"Look, I'll come straight to the point and I'm sorry to say this to you, Sam," Brianna continued, "but I can't talk to customers anymore."

"What, not as many?" Sam quizzed, "how many clients are you talking about here, Bree?"

"All of them Sam" Brianna responded firmly, "I don't want to speak to any of them."

Sam knew "don't want" and "can't' had two very different meanings. He sensed Brianna's reason was not that she couldn't but didn't want to. He was tempted to try a line he used in Late Arrears of "if I gave you $10,000 to speak to clients would you do it then" but prudently opted not to.

He also knew he couldn't simply cave into this demand without some consequences.

"Look" Sam responded, "I really feel for you Bree but you probably just need a break. After you come back from New Zealand, you may think differently. Have a good think when you are over there about whether or not you really want to leave the team."

"I don't want to leave the team" Brianna reacted, "I just don't want to talk to vulnerable clients."

"But if you're not going to speak to clients" Sam responded, "what-"I can do e-mail and administrative tasks," Brianna snapped.

"That is not going to work Bree and since VEW came along, our contact rates have soared, not to mention resolving the matters faster. Sam stressed, "your proposal will throw that all out of whack.

May as well throw VEW into the abyss. And just when our numbers are looking healthy, primarily thanks to VEW."

"You still have Mary and Logan to speak to clients," Brianna reasoned, "and Mary loves speaking to them. Plus, I am a very good administrator."

"That would be a bad precedent to set Bree" Sam responded.

"Well I just can't do it Sam" Brianna responded, tears welling, "and I don't want to lose my job."

Sam resigned himself to knowing he would not convince Brianna now that this was a bad idea and one he had no intention of approving. "OK, I'll tell you what" Sam said reassuringly, ""I'll speak to Bulldog," I am sure we can work something out."

'Thanks Sam" Brianna gushed. "How do you manage to cope? Nothing seems to bother you.

I'm going downstairs to grab a coffee. Do you want one?

"No thanks Bree," Sam replied, "keen for a cup of tea and jam doughnut, so I'll head to the TAB."

Brianna heads to the downstairs cafe as Sam makes his way to the TAB. He notices a busker he hasn't seen before warming up.

"Hey mate," Sam greets, "I haven't seen you here before." as Sam prompts a shaking of the hands, "Sam Crews."

"Ronnie Galah Sam," the busker replies. "Good timing because I am just about to kick off my first set."

"Brilliant, Ronnie" Sam enthused, "are you a mate of Paddy's?"

"One of my best me ol china," Ronnie replied. "Paddy's joining me in about an hour. You know I've never been on the dole, I've never paid for a root, and I've never been engaged."

"I'll alert the media" Sam responded sarcastically.

Sam takes a step back, and Ronnie does a thirty-second guitar solo before moving closer to the microphone stand. He then starts singing Pearl Jam's "Last Kiss".

https://www.youtube.com/watch?v=tNDWJ_KDkAc.

As Ronnie performs a crowd starts to gather around, many placing coins and notes in Ronnie's Akubra hat.

Chapter 18 Put Her On A Pip

"Put her on a PIP," Gavin thundered as he sat upright at his desk, directing his ire at Sam but loud enough for the entire Collections team seated nearby to hear him. Sam knew Gavin would not be receptive to the proposal to place Brianna on administrative tasks for the near future. But he thought his plan to gradually ease her back onto the phones to speak to vulnerable clients might help and Gavin would entertain the prospect of at least trying it for a couple of weeks.

"What, a performance improvement plan?" Sam reacted incredulously, "gee whiz Bulldog, that will go down like a lead balloon."

"We don't have the resources" Gavin responded, "to have someone on a full-time wage working part-time."

"We'll have Human Resources" Sam reacted "If we put her on a PIP. I can see Bree marching straight down to HR."

"That useless bunch," Gavin bemoaned. "Well she's gotta take calls, simple as that."

"I agree Bulldog" Sam responded, "and I introduced VEW Golf for that very reason but to put her on a PIP now, especially after she did lose a close friend to suicide, would be incredibly hard on her, not to mention a very bad look."

"It's a very bad look, someone refusing to talk to clients," Gavin countered, "Do you know how many people commit suicide each year?" he asked.

"No idea," Sam responded, "how many?"

"I don't know," Bulldog responded, "but I am sure it is a lot. Happens all the time but we don't cave in over it, we toughen up, we learn from it and become stronger. We knew she would face clients who have mental illness, domestic violence, terminal illness, and all the rest of them but her job is to deal with them."

"We could replace her," Sam reasoned.

"There are two hopes of that happening, mate: no hope and Bob Hope." Gavin reacted. "We are at our maximum head count and they won't give us any more; believe me I've tried. Hardship won't take her back, either. Also, Raj reckons you only need three people in Sensitive Matters, based on the numbers."

"I don't know where he is getting his numbers from" Sam countered, "even with the team we have now, we are flat out like a lizard drinking."

"You're not going soft on me are you Sam?" Gavin reacted with a smirk.

"Nought chance" Sam said indignantly. Sam agreed with Gavin and knew he wouldn't back down. But Bulldog didn't have to deal with Brianna, who Sam knew would also not back down.

Sam sensed Bulldog wanted Brianna to leave altogether, either voluntarily or constructively, and wanted her on a PIP, more because it was mandatory as part of managing someone out of the business, rather than improving performance. In Bulldog's eyes a PIP is not about coaching to produce greater competence in the role, it's a mechanism to get rid of someone.

"Good chat Bulldog" Sam uttered, "you make a lot of sense. I must go. Killarney is here today,

to give the team some training on how to better assist the vulnerable clients. Thanks for organising it."

"Perfect timing and another box ticked," Gavin cynically remarked, "who knows, this session may be perfect for Bree and she changes her mind, though I doubt it."

Inside the Skybox seated around the large corporate table are Mary and Logan with their eyes glued to the speaker at the front: Agnes Rowbottom. Though attendance for the three Sensitive Matters associates was mandatory, Brianna was a late withdrawal on the grounds she needed the time to prepare for her trip to New Zealand, The door flings open, and Sam walks in, "sorry for my tardiness folks, I was busy arranging for our calls to be taken by Late Arrears."

Agnes is a lifelong financial counsellor and in the last twenty years has been the head of a not-for-profit organisation named Thriving Communities Partnership (TPC) a subsidiary of a Christian church, which advises businesses on how to best deal with vulnerable clients. True to his word to the team, Sam approached Bulldog, who organised the session from TPC.

"....... we call it "Dealing With The Tough Stuff" Agnes declared, "after this two-hour session with me, I am confident you will all be better equipped to deal with challenging situations involving your vulnerable clients and in the broader community. Now," Agnes continued, "working with hardship and vulnerable customers is never easy. This is why understanding vulnerability is critical and knowing that a life event that impacts one person in a particular way may have a different effect on another. Let's start with the ABC.

Agnes turns the wallboard around to reveal in bold letters THE ABC MODEL. Underneath, ABC is broken down to "A - Antecedents. B - Behaviour. C - Consequences.

"People sometimes bemoan 'why did they do that'; Agnes continued, "or 'what was I thinking'. 'Why does he continue to come in to work late, even when I've told him to make sure he starts work on time?'. The ABC model is that a person's behaviours are caused by present events that occur before and after the behaviours have been performed."

Logan appears to be watching and listening but in truth, he is already bored and failing to digest Agnes' presentation, with a casual eye on the mobile phone he has hidden on his lap to catch an update on the World

Surf League, where an event took place in Hawaii overnight. He also decides to check Global's internal jobs' site with a none-too casual consideration to look for another role.

Mary, on the other hand, is engrossed with Agnes' delivery and revelations, lapping up every word. Sam has his eyes on all, taking in Agnes' words and aware of Logan's surfing shenanigans.

"So" Agnes continued, "antecedents are best explained as events that occur or are present before the person performs the behaviour. Behaviour is explained as what they did while Consequences are events that occur after and as a result of the behaviour."

"Can you give us an example?" Mary posed.

"Great question, Mary," Agnes responded, "and that was going to be my next piece. Think of when you are tired. Feeling tired is an antecedent for sleeping, sleeping is the behaviour and feeling rested the next day is a consequence of sleeping."

Sam gets an alert on his phone that he was sent an SMS. It's from Logan, who looks at him from the other side of the table. "This is boring me witless."

On level 3 Mark Bryers and Adeel Makhur are at it again after a loan application, via a valued broker, was declined.

"I'm telling you Adeel," Mark stressed, "this loan needs to be approved. The client is good for it, and it's been referred by our number one broker."

"But the client's credit score is pitiful" Adeel reacted, "he has three defaults and a court judgement. There is no way I can approve it."

An hour later after completing her presentation, Agnes left the Skybox to be replaced by a financial counsellor from Killarney Care, Marie Salizzo, a middle-aged lady with long, grey hair, sharply dressed in a burgundy business suit. Behind her, and in full view of Logan and Mary, is a large whiteboard

Listen

Empathise

Acknowledge

Respond

Notify

Three hours later, long after the Vulnerable Client training finished and the Sensitive Matters team had finished for the day, Mary was sitting at a table in the TAB, in the corner, on her own, away from other patrons and with a smile on her face. It was the one spot where horse-racing and sport didn't feature on the television screens in the vicinity, rather the sole screen dedicated to music.

Mary was thinking about how much she loved Killarney's presentation and the compassion and understanding they expressed for people facing financial and life difficulties. She thought of when she initially learned she would be in the Sensitive Matters team, recalling Sam's comment about choosing a job you love and you won't work a day in your life. And though she didn't choose Sensitive Matters, she felt that adage applied to her. The Killarney training session reinforced that. Mary was feeling more emboldened than ever to go the extra mile to help the vulnerable.

Mary looked up at the television and could see a new video on the YouTube channel emerging.

As she does, a text message comes through on her phone. It's from Logan: "Hey Mary, there is a job going in our DEI team, I reckon it's just what you've been looking for, it has your name written all over it."

Mary digests the message, ponders its contents for a few seconds then looks back up at the television screen where a picture of odd-looking, alien-type figures appear as a voice sings the words:

Lordy don't leave me - All by myself.

Lordy don't leave me - All by myself.

Mary thought of some of Global's vulnerable clients, primarily Ingrid Pavlich and Tara Baldwin and how she was not going to abandon them as she sat back to watch Moby's "In This World".

https://www.youtube.com/watch?v=5wrwcEZ3Btw

Chapter 19 Repossess For Success

The following morning, as the clock ticks past 11 o'clock, Sam emerges from the TAB, armed with a Win and Place, striding boldly back to the office when his attention is grabbed by the sound from The Burrow. A piercing soprano voice, Magic Flute-like, rang out across the Corso and when Sam looked over; he saw two ladies singing "Aria - Ode To Humanity" by Yanni with Sherese supporting on drums and Ronnie on guitar.

https://www.youtube.com/watch?v=yGQTygjOBhQ

There is no immediate sign of Paddy until Sam notices him immersed in the crowd.

"Gee whiz Paddy," Sam said, "this is a bit of a change for The Burrow."

"Remember the Two Tenors from the other day?" Paddy posed.

"Of course" Sam responded, "they did that spiffing rendition of Run To You."

"Well they told some of their mates at the Con and a heap of them now want to perform" Paddy said.

"Wow Paddy" Sam said, "you've got them coming from everywhere."

"How did it go with your missus?" Paddy asked.

"All right," Sam said as he noticed a message from Bulldog telling him a meeting scheduled for later in the day has been brought forward, giving him another ten minutes until it starts. "I realised that not only have I never brought Vincent to The Burrow, you've never met him. Hard to believe. I guess this fatherhood caper and dealing with vulnerable clients has made my thinking go a bit skew-whiff"

"That's great Sam" Paddy remarked candidly, "but rather than feel sorry for yourself, what are you going to do about it?"

"Touché" Sam said smilingly, "I must skedaddle, but I will hopefully see you a bit later and Abbey is my ex-missus," keen to get in the last word as he heads off.

"Make sure you are here at around five," Paddy yelled, "Ronnie will be on, and he is on fire at

Present."

Sam makes his way to the Skybox, where the meeting is to be held with Bulldog, Stuart and Eric. Sam has not been given any details for the appointment but has an inkling it will be to discuss how to make greater advancements in Sensitive Matters, notably a faster resolution of cases and lowering the arrears within the SM portfolio. Sam hadn't told Bulldog about his VEW Golf model, which, in its early stages, was starting to yield rewards. Sam was looking forward to sharing this positive development and as he approached the room he noticed Gavin seated in discussion with Stuart and Eric and was about to enter when out of nowhere, Renita appeared.

"Hello Sam" Renita smiles, "how are you?"

"Going well thanks Renita, "Sam replied, "Sensitive cases are mounting but we're getting resolutions more quickly now." as they stood outside the Skybox.

"Sensitive cases aside," Renita pressed, "how are you going?"

Sam can see that Gavin and co are waiting for him. Gavin looks at Sam, raises his right arm then looks at his wristwatch to infer Sam needs to get a move on.

"I'm really well thanks Renita, "Sam replied, "I'd better go and not keep the crew waiting but great seeing you."

"Likewise Sam" Renita replied, "let's catch up for a coffee."

"Even better, a daily double at the TAB, leave it with me" Sam responded as he entered the meeting room.

"Leave what with you?" Gavin enquired as Stuart was in the process of connecting his laptop to the giant screen at the front of the room.

"Just about catching up for a cuppa Bulldog," Sam replied as observed the big screen while sitting down to see, in bold capital letters:

SENSITIVE MATTERS - CARS TO REPOSSESS

"So how was the training Sam," Bulldog said, "worked out well for the team?"

Sam had an inkling that Bulldog raised the subject merely as a tick-the-box exercise, rather than genuinely caring about his team's wellbeing, but settled on Bulldog being genuinely interested.

"It had its moments, Bulldog" Sam replied, "plenty of good stuff there, which should make it easier for the team to deal with vulnerable clients. Lots of emphasis on having empathy."

"Yeah it's the in word these days Sammy" Bulldog said, "though empathy is not an absolute, there are times when empathy does not apply. Being empathetic has its place but not every single time. We have customers who have no intention of paying and come up with sob stories, and we are at fault for not having empathy, give me a break."

The Skybox door opens, and Johnny Kep makes a hasty entry. "Sorry I'm late" Johnny apologised, "Pymbles had private buyers for 2 cars for which I had to provide our valuation."

"We're all very busy" Gavin uttered, "so let's get straight into it and not waste any time. I got Raj and his workflow team to give me a list of contracts which are 91 days and more in arrears. As you know, the index has hit 0.7 which is unacceptable and we are going to look at each of these contracts and unless there is a damn good reason not to, I want repossession agents out there this week.

And none of this time to sell nonsense; they can voluntarily surrender the asset for us to sell at public auction or we enforce repossession. I do not believe in time to sell, for the client anyway. Anyone who says they are looking to sell it privately is just buying time to keep the car and not make payments.

After this meeting I want you Sam and Johnny to engage with Scholes, speak to John Scholes if you have to. After our meeting last week he has given his agents very clear instructions to treat these sensitive cases with more care."

Though this meeting with Bulldog was unexpected, Sam reflected and realised this should have come as no surprise. Repossessions in Sensitive Matters had become the exception, thanks in part to the strong cases made by Mary to refrain from doing so, for the time being at least. While his competitive nature didn't like it that Bulldog was the one to initiate this meeting, he felt a sense of relief that he could now push back on Mary's pleas with greater authority.

"As we all know," Gavin added, "the longer we delay a repossession, the more the arrears index goes up and the more the value of the asset, a depreciating asset, goes down. Time is on the march. Now, the first contract we are going to look at is Sam-"

"Before that, Bulldog" Stuart interjects, "shall we mention the twenty loans where the balance is less than the valuation?"

"Good point Stu," Bulldog reacted, "I almost forgot. So Sam, Stuart has uncovered a list of loans where the remaining balances are less than what the asset is worth. So the plan of attack is for your team to explain to these debtors that after the vehicle is sold, whatever surplus funds are there will be refunded to them, which will enable them to buy another car outright - with no debt. A brilliant strategy and kudos to Stu for coming up with it."

Sam sat digesting the proposal, surprised there were this many loans in Sensitive Matters where the value of the asset essentially dwarfed the balance of the loan. He figured any surplus is likely to be minimal and not enough to buy another car. As Sam was about to question the idea, Bulldog interrupted his train of thought.

"Let's get cracking" a buoyant Bulldog said, "what have you got for us Stu?"

"The first loan is for an Ingrid Pavlich, $14,000 and 388 days in arrears," Stuart announced.

"Sam, Johnny, this is an absolute mess. We repossessed the car; it's been in the garage but still not put up for auction. What the hell is happening?" Gavin demanded.

"It's a bit convoluted" Sam responded. "Mrs Pavlich has a terminal illness - cancer - three children under the age of ten, she is paralysed from the waist down and uses a wheelchair; she had the car modified to accommodate this. She lives in country Victoria, three hundred kilometres from Melbourne and the car is the only means of transport she has to get to the hospital."

"Last payment was six months ago and the balance is forty-five grand," Stuart interjected.

"And the valuation is $30-35k," Johnny added.

"All right" Gavin said, "what's the recovery plan for her, Sam?'

"Her recovery plan" Sam answered, "is for her husband to get a job, hopefully sometime soon."

"What, the husband is unemployed too" Gavin snapped.

"Both Mrs Pavlich and her husband are on Centrelink" Sam advised, "their only source of income."

"Why is the husband not working?" Gavin asked, "I can understand that she isn't, though plenty of disabled people have jobs, but what's his excuse?"

"He's essentially a full-time carer, for the client and their three children, who are all under ten years of age" Sam reiterated. "However, once he returns to full-time employment, I am reasonably confident full rental repayments will resume."

"Like smoke Sam" Gavin rebuffed, "if they return to full rental payments in the next year I'll give you a gold clock. I appreciate they are in a lot of strife but that doesn't entitle them to a free car.

We are charitable but we are not a charity. Immediately to auction."

Sam knew there was no point in arguing. While to many the tactics employed by Gavin here looked like an ambush, this was his modus operandi, attack in numbers. Sam had been on the other side right behind Gavin when in Late Arrears and it was his first experience of being on the receiving end. But it didn't bother him because he knew Gavin had a point, one for which he did not have a feasible and reasonable counter. As Sam nodded, Stuart moved straight onto the next contract.

"OK" Stuart said, "the next on the list is contract # 1275-

Back at the Sensitive Matters domain, Logan and Mary were discussing their portfolios and the new list of accounts received that day.

"Gosh Logan," Mary said, "a bit of a rarity. A loan coded to my portfolio today is up-to-date."

"So why do we have it?" Logan queried.

"Mental illness," Mary answered. "Jarryd Breeden, 41 years old, lives with his mother, unemployed for the last three years, only income has been from Centrelink while his mother is on the old-aged pension and according to his financial counsellor, 'Jarryd struggles to get out of bed in the morning'.

"Yet his loan is up-to-date" Logan said.

"Quite remarkable" Mary added. "It's with us because the financial counsellor has asked us to waive the remaining debt, just over $3k. I'm going to make a strong case to Sam to accede to the request."

"Here's one I haven't seen before, Mary," Logan revealed, "the client's name is Dorothy Hunt and it's been coded to us from Customer Service under Elder Abuse. I'm not even sure what that means."

"You obviously weren't listening at the Killarney session" Mary replied, "they spent a bit of time on that very subject."

"Yeah, well," Logan uttered, "those guys bored me witless."

"So, look it up Logan" Mary responded impudently.

"I'm a step ahead of you, Mary" Logan responded, "I already have and it says here that it is 'someone controlling your ability to get, use or keep your money or economic resources. People who use coercive control might use economic and financial abuse as part of their abusive behaviour.' My goodness, hats off to the Customer Service agent who knew to code it to this."

Car Loans was a slightly misleading title as it wasn't just cars which were financed: trucks, caravans and even tractors were also on the books. This was the case with Dorothy Hunt, for whom loans for a semi-trailer truck and a tractor were financed. The applications stated Dorothy owned a farm and used the vehicles for this purpose. The farm had reportedly been hit with a severe drought and now the two contracts were three months in arrears.

Normally this would be a standard collections matter but concerns were raised when it was discovered that all contact since inception had been with the client's son, Michael Hunt, and that when the loans were created, Dorothy was 80 years old; she is now 86.

"I am going to have to speak to Sam about this one"

Logan remarked, "what were the credit team thinking when they approved this loan?"

Mary being Mary couldn't help herself, she needed to look at this account. After peering over Logan's shoulder to see the contract number, she quickly brought up the details on her screen.

"I assume you looked at the application, Logan" Mary mused as she clicked on the loan documents.

"I had a look Mary" Logan replied, "couldn't really see anything untoward, I never do. They always seem to have valid reasons for approving the most questionable loans. This one looked fine to me."

Mary's eyes enlarged as she noticed something on the application. "It looks like," Mary noted, "Dorothy Hunt came on the scene late. This loan was initially for a Michael Hunt but he failed the credit criteria however, before it was declined, Dorothy Hunt was added as a borrower. It appears the broker contacted the sales team and Mark Bryers got involved. Next thing you know Dorothy Hunt is on the loan."

"So they are co-borrowers then," Logan observed.

"No, Michael Hunt was removed altogether, and looking at his credit file at the time I am not surprised, terrible," Mary responded, "but that left one borrower: Dorothy Hunt is solely liable."

"Ooh" Logan said, "I almost forgot. Did you get my message about the DEI role?"

"Yes I did, Logan" Mary replied, "thanks for thinking of me."

"It's a lay down misère Mary" Logan said, "this is exactly what you've always wanted, and knowing you I am sure you have already submitted your application."

Mary smiled without verbally responding before returning to view Dorothy Hunt's file.

Three hours later, long after his meeting with Bulldog and Stuart finished, Sam called it a day at Global and heeded Paddy's call to watch Ronnie perform. As he approaches The Burrow he observes the lack of activity with the only person there being Sherese, who appears to be reading a book. As he gets closer, he gets a tap on the shoulder.

"Good to see you me ol china" Ronnie beams as they both embrace.

"Paddy told me you were performing something special" Sam reacted, "so there was nought chance I'd miss it, though it's just passed 5 o'clock, and there doesn't seem to be much happening."

Ronnie ditched Sam and quickly entered The Burrow and strapped his guitar on as Sherese discarded her book and sat at the drums. Both were preparing to sing, judging by the microphones they each had standing in front of them. Ronnie starts the guitar and after the introductory chords, he sings

"Ain't No Sunshine" with Sherese on back-up vocals. As they perform a few of the growing crowd outside The Burrow start to clap to the music and cheer them on.

Ain't no sunshine when she's gone

It's not warm when she's away

Ain't no sunshine when she's gone

And she's always gone too long

Anytime she goes away

Ain't no sunshine - David Cassidy

Chapter 20 The Auction

Johnny arrives at Sam's desk in the Sensitive Matters domain. It's 5.30 on a Friday evening and Mary and Logan were both out the door when the inbound lines closed half-an-hour earlier. It has been a hectic and exhausting week for the team, and they are all looking forward to the weekend.

"Ready to go?" Johnny asks.

"Absolutely," Sam replies as he logs out of his computer and heads towards the stairs with Johnny.

As much as Sam is looking forward to the weekend, he is looking forward to this particular Friday evening more. It's the Pymbles Luxury Car Auction, an event that happens six times a year and which Johnny has attended more times than he can remember. It will be Sam's first.

It also happens to fall on the weekend Sam is down to look after Vincent, however, Abbey agreed to have him until Saturday morning to enable Sam to enjoy the auction.

Pymbles orchestrates three general car auctions every week, each of which consists of over one hundred vehicles put up for sale and are considered by most as the leading auctioneers in the country.

Punters show up in large numbers to attend in person but there is also plenty of on-line activity. The jewel in the crown for Pymbles, though is the Luxury Vehicle Auction.

All of Pymbles' auctions have one common denominator: the bulk of their offerings are repossessions by financial institutions. They also cater for state governments and insurance companies, but repossessions rule and their best client is Global Bank. On this occasion, Global had twelve vehicles entered and, after the troubling management of Angela Rankin's loan, Sam was particularly interested to see how this would materialise. Bulldog also thought it would be a good opportunity for Sam to become better acquainted with the Pymbles staff and appreciate the other side of the mercantile and auction facets. But most importantly, Gavin believed it would lead to a greater number of repossessions in the Sensitive Matters portfolio.

Johnny's love and expertise for valuing cars is not matched by his desire to drive them, he prefers getting around on a motorised scooter. But on occasions like today, where he is compelled to drive, he takes his 2006 Toyota Camry. As he and Sam make their way to the auction he turns on the car CD. "OK Sam, you have three choices: Nirvana, Elvis Presley or The Korgis."

"Well, I have heard of Nirvana and Elvis," Sam responded, but The Korgis is a new one. What are they, a rap group?"

"They are from the 1980s," Johnny responded, "I don't think rap was a factor back then."

"Let's go with the Korgis then, Johnny," Sam enthused, "I'm always a fan of listening to something new, even if it is old."

Gavin and Stuart had already been at the Pymbles premises for an hour when Sam and Johnny arrived. The auction had also attracted plenty of prospective bidders scattered around the showroom inspecting the vehicles on offer. Global were given a private viewing suite with an endlessly stocked bar of the finest beers and wine combined with a range of food on which to dine. While this was Sam's first attendance, it had happened countless times before for Gavin, Stuart and Eric who, unlike Johnny who was a teetotaller, were typically taking advantage of the endless flow of food and alcohol.

"Here you go Sam" Gavin said as he handed him a bottle of Stella Artois, "get that into ya."

Johnny approached the fridge and plucked a beer for himself

"Knock me dead if I'm a jack-in-the-box," Gavin blurted, "Johnny Kep on the beers."

"Non-alcoholic Bulldog" Johnny explained, "nought percent."

Stuart and Eric looked mockingly at Gavin who ignored them both. While Bulldog was a pronounced boozer, no matter what time of the day, he held a begrudging respect for Johnny's abstinence approach.

"Hey Sam, let me show you some of our cars up for auction, including yours from Sensitive."

Johnny offered.

"Sure," Sam replied, "let's go."

"Well wait until you see some of these cars" added Johnny, as he walked into the showroom, displaying over a hundred luxury vehicles, with most getting plenty of attention from prospective bidders. "Whilst I hope for big prices for our vehicles, I reckon there will be a few bargains here tonight. You may even want to bid for one yourself."

Sam followed John to the display room. The range of cars are impressive," Sam said, "but so is the turnout of people. There must be a lot of money around."

"You'll find the majority of people here are from dealerships" Johnny responded. "There are a few punters, but not many compared to the dealers."

Sam was in awe of the vast number of high-quality vehicles, all looking to be in pristine condition, Pymbles had done a great job in preparing them. There were Mercedes, BMW, Bentley.

Jaguar, Alfa Romeo, Porsche and more. He also noticed a VW and a Ford F-150.

"I thought this was supposed to be only for luxury cars?" Sam questioned.

"It is," Johnny responded, "but the definition of a luxury car is one which has an LCT worth more than $80k."

"What's an LCT?" Sam asked.

"Luxury car tax," Johnny replied. "I wouldn't think too deeply about it Sam, LCT has a few variations to it like fuel efficiency but just accept that all these cars up for auction tonight officially fall under the luxury car label."

A 2022 Lexus catches Johnny's eye. "One of ours?" surmised Sam.

"Yes" replied Johnny, "one of our better ones."

Bulldog appears behind them, "what do you reckon, Johnny, your reserves will hold up?"

"Which one, the prices on the vehicles or his energy levels?" Sam quipped.

"It'll kick off soon boys" Gavin advised, "so before we get into it, Sam I want to introduce you to some of our hosts, get to know a few more of the stakeholders."

"See you back there Johnny" said Sam, "thanks for the guided tour."

When Sam returned, Stuart was already looking well on his way to inebriation. The auction hadn't even started and Stuart's glazed drinking look was emerging. He was talking to a Pymbles executive when Gavin interrupted them.

"Gerry Smyth," Gavin prompted, "this is Sam Crews, manager of our Sensitive Matters Department."

"Nice to meet you Sam," Gerry said as they shook hands, "make yourself at home here, have whatever you want, it's all on us."

"Thanks Gerry" Sam replied, "I can't get over how impressive this all looks."

"Well, it's going to get a lot more impressive Sam" Gerry beamed, "wait until you see some of the prices we bring in. We have the best auctioneers in the country and they know how to entice somebody to bid."

At that moment the first car rolled out, with the auctioneer taking the stand.

"All right folks," boomed the auctioneer, "welcome to Pymbles' 38th Luxury Car Auction where the most prestigious and luxurious cars from all over Australia will be on offer for you to bid for and, if you are the lucky bidder, buy."

Johnny joined them. "Here we go fellas, this is the first of our dozen."

The car about to be auctioned was a 2022 Porsche Cayenne for which there appeared to be considerable interest. After the first bid of $40,000 the auctioneer was kept busy with 2 punters trading bids. The final bid came in at $95,000.

"Just checking with the sellers there Sir" said the auctioneer who looked over at John who gave a subtle nod.

"Sold for $95,000......."

Bulldog, like Stuart, had consumed his fair share of beers but it rarely appeared to have an impact on his cognisance, especially when it was business related.

"Didn't we put a reserve of $100k on that one Johnny?"

"You are right Bulldog," Johnny replied, "but this is the second time we've put it to auction, last time it stopped at $90k, so I used my discretion."

"What's the shortfall?" Stuart asked

"After the auction deductions,, freight costs, and agent fees, it'll be about $20k," Johnny replied.

"Nah, that's fair enough," Gavin said, "good work."

Sam was at the adjoining table, engaged in conversation with Gerry

"That car was repossessed in Townsville." Gerry mentioned.

"So why did it end up in Sydney?' Sam asked, "don't you have an auction facility in Townsville?"

"We do," Gerry replied, "in fact we have eighteen auction premises throughout Australia but we discerned this is the best auction house for it and is likely to give us an optimum price."

"I imagine it would have been costly to transport the car from Townsville to Sydney" Sam suggested.

Bulldog was keeping an eye and ear on their conversation and quickly interjected before Gerry could answer. "Yes but it all comes off the sale price and gets charged to the client," Gavin advised, "we don't cop any of it."

"What if the client says no and they don't want to incur the freight cost and auction it in the city where it resided?" Sam queried.

"It's not their call, solely at our discretion"; Gavin replied. "Remember, this is only happening because the debtor didn't pay what was due."

The night wore on and Sam was taking turns drinking beer and water, conscious he had a big weekend ahead looking after Vincent. An inebriated Stuart had been put in a taxi and gone home while, despite downing at least a dozen beers on the night, Gavin remained in a reasonably perceptive state. Pymbles were nearing the end of the auction with just five cars left when Johnny appeared.

"Here it is, Sam," Johnny said excitedly.

The car emerging was a Ford Mustang which made Sam think back to the conversation he had with Ali. He then thought of Jenny Johannsen, Angela Rankin's mum. He suddenly felt emotional.

"This is the car from the chick who killed herself." Gavin injudiciously blurted.

Sam's emotions worsened. He was now feeling sick in the stomach and couldn't understand why. While Gavin's callous remark didn't help, it wasn't a factor and he'd known about this matter for a while and felt completely at ease throughout. This surely was a good outcome: one less contract in the Sensitive Matters portfolio, will contribute to reducing the arrears index, and if there are surplus funds after the sale, which is likely, he would be in for an augmented quarterly bonus.

Sam didn't hear or see the auctioneer, nor did he notice Gavin and Eric celebrating the sale price of $58,000. He was in another world, thinking of a smiling Angela Rankin after being told she would have three months off without payments, then her mum, Jenny Johannsen who, though devastated at her loss, could not have been more helpful to Sam and the team in returning the Mustang.

"SAM" Gavin imported in a raised voice, "for the fourth time, let's grab a beer. Celebrate your Win." Sam looked blankly at Gavin then turned his attention to Johnny who was writing down the particulars of the sale at the table next to him, before reacting to Gavin. "I will in a minute Bulldog, I just have to grab something from the car."

Gavin and Eric headed to the fridge as Sam asked Johnny for his car keys, which he duly obliged. Once in the car Sam dialled his mobile phone and waited for a response.

"Don't think for one minute," Abbey answered, "that you are not having Vincent in the morning.

I thought this might happen."

"And a very good evening to you too, Abbey" Sam quipped, "that is the last thing on my mind.

In fact it's the opposite, I am very much looking forward to spending the weekend with Vince, taking him to the park and checking out his soccer skills."

There is a pause from Abbey, taken aback by Sam's comments. "So, how is the auction going?"

"Not that great Abbey" Sam responded, "I thought I would be having a whale of a time but I couldn't help but think of how those vehicles got there in the first place. Especially Amanda Rankin."

"Who is Amanda Rankin?" Abbey asked.

Sam went on to explain how she was a client who committed suicide and how he wondered if it could've been avoided. As Abbey listens intently and empathetically Johnny is talking to Gavin.

"That's our twelve cars done and dusted Bulldog," Johnny said, "I'm going to head home."

"Splendid work, Johnny" Gavin reacted, "every one of the cars sold at or slightly above reserve. Your valuations were spot on; your blood is worth bottling."

Johnny smiled, bade farewell, and headed to his car. He could see Sam was on his phone, so stopped walking to allow Sam some space.

"Do you remember when Vincent was born?" Sam recalled to Abbey, "and I'd come home from work and get to the door and hear him crying, so would retreat to the car and listen to music?"

"Of course," Abbey replied.

"It's not too dissimilar now" Sam added. "I'm not very good at dealing with misery when it hits me directly. And the thing is, the team goes through a lot worse than me, they are the ones on the front line, speaking to people who often don't have a prayer but desperately need the car."

"It's a tough job you've got" Abbey sympathised, "not many people could do it."

"Yeah" Sam bemoaned, "I guess. And it's gonna get a lot tougher."

Sam notices Johnny standing a few metres away and realises he needs to wrap up the call.

"Look Abbey, I have to go. I don't want to, I've really enjoyed our chat and thanks for being such a great listener but Johnny's here and it's time to leave this place."

They both say goodbye and Sam quickly alights from the car.

"Sorry about that, Johnny boy" Sam said as he tossed the keys to him, "I was just having a chat with Abbey."

"How is she?" Johnny reacted, "I haven't seen her in ages" as they each climbed into the car.

"She's good," Sam said before thinking about his response. "Actually I don't know, I forgot to ask, I was too wrapped up in my little world."

"Man, I wouldn't be a parent for all the tea in China; I'm too selfish," Johnny said as he turned on the car ignition. "But of course, you are a dad, so you don't have a choice. And Abbey, gosh, just think of what Abbey has given up. Abbey is a great girl."

As they drive off, Johnny turns on the radio while Sam looks ahead thinking of Johnny's last words and how, before Vincent was born, he thought exactly the same thing. The song "Everybody's Gotta Learn Sometime" by The Korgis is playing.

"Change your heart ....

https://www.youtube.com/watch?v=kuuSlHw2Dw8

Chapter 21 Veterans Voice

"It's good news for the Blues

Now there's no more time to lose

Cos we're hot on the trail

And there's no way we're gonna fail

So get your coat on

And get moving

Sam was fast asleep when the Everton team song began on the morning of a new working week. Lying next to him in bed was his son, Vincent, also sound asleep, after spending the weekend together. The loud Everton chant woke them both instantly. Thinking it was 6 a.m., a groggy Sam habitually jumped out of bed, hitting his head on the dressing table in the process.

"Gee whiz" Sam muttered, "I must've really overslept," as the Everton song suddenly stopped.

"But" as he looked at Vincent, "there is no better way to start the day than hear Everton play.

You will support an EPL team one day son, hopefully it is Everton but whatever team that is, I guarantee you will love the Everton song."

Sam then looked at the alarm, puzzled that the song didn't continue to play until the end, as it always has, only to see the time as 5.33 confusing him even more. Sam checked on Vincent who, at this point, was sitting up, wide-eyed and smiling. It then dawned on him: it wasn't the alarm that went off, it was his phone, remembering he had changed the ringtone a few days earlier.

"Gosh," Sam uttered, "who is ringing at five thirty in the morning" as he checked the number, one he didn't recognise before ringing the caller back.

"Good morning Sam, it's Renita and sorry to call you so early."

"Not at all, Renita," Sam reacted, "you can ring me any time."

"There's been an incident," Renita explained, "I need you in the office ASAP."

Sam knew something serious must've happened for Renita to ring him but his first thoughts were for Vincent and preparing for, and taking to, school.

"I just have one slight problem Renita" Sam remarked, "I have to take my son to school, and they don't open until 8."

"You have a son," Renita exclaimed in a surprised tone, "I didn't know Sam, my apologies. Of course, he comes first. I'll delay the start of the meeting to 8.30 so I'll see you in the Manly office when you get there."

"I should be there by then Renita," Sam responded, "maybe even a fraction earlier." As he hung up the phone he promptly headed to the bathroom, only to notice Vincent gazing at him. "Who was that Dad?" he asked.

"Someone from work, son," Sam replied. "Let's get ready for our respective days ahead," as he plucked a towel from the cupboard and tossed it to Vincent. "You have a shower whilst I ring your mother."

Vincent sprang from the bed as Sam scoured the names on his phone before he came to what he was looking for: Abbey. Anxious to know what the "incident" was, he thought he would ask Abbey to take Vincent to school to enable him to get to work earlier. He was about to dial the number when he paused before tossing the mobile on his bed. He realised he had to deal with this himself.

Hours later, at 8.25, over at Global's Manly office, the self-assured Gavin, accompanied by Stuart, marches into the Skybox to find Renita sitting at the table, along with a lawyer, Hayden Gensic, from the Car Loans legal team.

"Good morning Renita, lads" Gavin uttered, "glad to see legal is here; how are you Hayden?"

"I'm all right thanks Gavin" Hayden replied.

"Gavin, Stuart," Renita acknowledged.

A slightly dishevelled Johnny Kep walks into the room. "Good morning all" Johnny uttered, "I hope I haven't missed anything."

"Good morning, John" Renita greeted. "We were just about to get started. Sam will join us a little later as he had a pre-arranged errand to run."

Prior to Sam's conversation this morning with Renita, Johnny was the only person at Global who knew about Vincent. He wondered if Renita was told, aware Sam does not want anyone at his workplace to know, especially Bulldog, believing such a revelation would impede his career progression. Bulldog is a father himself, married for seven years, which ended in two children and a divorce. He also has little to no contact with his son and daughter who both live with their mother in New Zealand. Johnny is Sam's closest confidante at Global and knows he can be trusted.

Before entering the office, Johnny took a moment to buy a win and place from the TAB. The win, a cup of Earl Grey tea, was for himself, while the Place, a chocolate chip biscuit, was for Sam but after Renita revealed Sam would be coming later, he changed tack.

"I thought you might like this Renita" Johnny offered as he gave her the Place. "They say good-hearted people like chocolate chip biscuits." Renita smiled and thanked Johnny as she gratefully accepted the cookie, bringing a snigger from Gavin.

"It's fortunate Stuart and I do not eat sweets, eh Johnny" he commented.

"I knew that Bulldog," Johnny quipped, "otherwise, I'd have bought you one too."

"Let's get started shall we" Renita exclaimed. "overnight, Global Car Loans was plastered all over social media and, unfortunately, not in a good light. A car was repossessed from a war veteran, a decorated soldier who served two tours of Afghanistan and suffering Post Traumatic Stress Disorder. The repossession occurred at the mental health facility where the client was hospitalised."

"We weren't aware of the PTSD; we were only made aware of it when it was revealed on social media." Gavin reacted defiantly.

"Surely you were made aware of the PTSD when the car was repossessed," Hayden interjected, "the repossession happened at a mental facility."

Gavin looked at Stuart who shrugged his shoulders. Johnny, looking shell-shocked, realised this is something of which he should have been across but wasn't. He racked his brain thinking of recently collected vehicles and recalled a Ford Ranger.

"I wasn't aware" Johnny responded, "do you have the name of the client?"

'Ronald Jacka," Hayden replied, ""Scholes provided a very detailed report" as he peered at his laptop.

Johnny was confused. He was across all repossession instructions delivered to Scholes and did not recall any telling them to attend a mental facility. He promptly opened his laptop, eager to read the report. "I am fairly certain we told the agent to attend the client's home, not a mental facility," as he clicked on the e-mail.

"You are correct Johnny, the agent was told to attend Mr Jacka's home," Renita clarified.

"It started out at the home," Stuart said "but once Scholes determined he didn't live there they did some digging."

"What sort of 'digging'?" Renita asked.

"The agent showed up at the client's home and he wasn't there," Gavin explained. "It happens often. And, as per standard procedure, the agent spoke to a neighbour to try and get more information and was told by the neighbour that the client hadn't been seen in a number of weeks. Nobody seemed to know where he or the car were."

"Explain the process to me Gavin," Renita insisted "in the event the client and/or vehicle are not at the nominated address, they report back to us for further instructions, right?"

"Sometimes," Gavin replied, "other times they might conduct their own skip-tracing to find the client themselves. It's quite common where our own collections teams cannot find the client so Scholes, which has a superb skip-tracing team, does it for us. These guys are the best in the business, as they further showed here by finding this client."

"There's two grand gone," Johnny muttered to himself, out of the others' hearing range, aware this is the average fee Scholes charges for conducting skip-tracing.

"OK" Renita pressed, "so they do their skip-tracing, find the client and then ring us?"

"Not necessarily," Stuart interjected. "As Gavin said, Scholes are the best in the business and the general instructions are to repossess the asset. They know what is required."

"Well not in this case Stuart" Renita snapped.

"In fairness, Renita," Stuart responded, "we didn't know this client suffered from PTSD."

"Scholes didn't know either," Gavin added, "at least not at first. They only found that out when they showed up at the mental facility."

Hayden looked at Renita, slightly bewildered by Gavin and Stuart's line of thinking and defending the Scholes agents. Hayden then quoted the report.

"After the agent went to the mental hospital, he witnessed the asset parked in the hospital driveway. From there, he entered the hospital building and spoke to a nurse at the front desk who confirmed that Mr Jacka was a patient there. The agent then proceeded to the ward and found the client lying in a bed. The agent approached the client, informed him of the intention to repossess the vehicle, and got the client to sign a release form.... "

A brief silence descended upon the room.

"Before everyone else gets wind of this, we need to get things back to what they were prior to the repossession" Renita stressed, "so we need Sam to contact the client and arrange to return the vehicle to him. I'll deal with Veterans Voice and the media."

Gavin stayed silent, though inside, he was livid, not because of the treatment given to Mr Jacka but that we would be returning a vehicle after being repossessed without the arrears being paid. In his eyes this was heresy but he knew not to make his feelings known to Renita. He wanted her to believe they were on the same page.

"This Veterans Voice is a pretty impressive outfit" Johnny interjected. "I'm just looking at their website and it states they are a not-for-profit organisation which provides holistic support services to enable present and past Australian Defence Force personnel, and their families, to lead meaningful civilian lives. It talks about stress, depression, trauma, PTSD_"

"Yeah thanks Johnny," a slightly peeved Gavin interrupted, "we get the picture."

"A good cause to donate a few bucks I reckon" Johnny added.

"I'll also be meeting with Scholes today, to discuss what happened and ensure there is never a repeat." Stuart said

"Good" Renita reacted, "there won't be a repeat with Scholes because that's the last time they do any business with us."

"That's a bit harsh" Gavin reacted. "They have saved us millions over the years, and they make one little oversight and now you want to get rid of them."

Renita wasn't happy with Gavin's stance but didn't overtly show it. "For the moment, that is a secondary issue," Renita replied, "you and I can discuss that later."

'How is he?" Johnny asked.

"How is who?" Stuart reacted.

"Ronald Jacka," Johnny answered

The room again went silent. Nobody had thought to find out. The door opened and in waltzed Sam.

"Greetings folks," Sam exclaimed, "sorry I am late, I hope we are all in good spirits and rearing to go. What have I missed?" as he notices everyone there is dressed in a business suit, with the exception of Johnny who is wearing a Billabong open-necked shirt, black jeans and green socks. Sam was initially in two minds on what to wear that morning: smart casual or the more time-consuming suit and tie. He was glad he opted for the latter.

"Perfect timing, Sam" Renita responded, "you and Johnny have a very important job to do today."

"Well let's hope he is OK," Johnny continued, "I imagine he will be a lot better when he hears he will be getting his car back."

Gavin and Stuart get up from the desk and leave the room as Renita and Hayden proceed to explain the situation to Sam. After the discussion Sam heads to the TAB, hankering for a daily double.

As he darts across the Corso, Ronnie Galah, who is tuning his guitar, notices him."

"Sammy boy" Ronnie shouts, "get me a win and place, will you me ol china" grinning broadly.

Sam gives Ronnie a thumbs up and walks into the TAB in, which a sizeable crowd has formed, most of whom have their eyes glued to the three large television screens all beaming live the English Premier League clash between Manchester United and Manchester City. After ordering a Daily Double and a Win and Place he starts engaging with the supporters and notices Ali is there clad in a Manchester United scarf.

"Hey Ali" Sam greeted, "I didn't know you were a Man U fan."

"My whole life," Ali responded, "and my father's whole life and his father's whole life. How's Sensitive Matters going?"

"Lots of headaches, Ali" Sam replied, "but we are making progress."

"Well, you have a great team for it" Ali said, "especially Bree, she is so good, we all really miss her."

"Really?" Sam quizzed, recalling her mid-year report indicated they would be glad to see her go.

"Of course" Ali responded with a tinge of indignity, "and she'd still be there if it weren't for Bulldog."

Sam's focus is now solely on Ali, ignoring the game and his order. "What do you mean?" he asked.

"Bulldog pressured her to decline Hardship a lot more, put all these conditions to be approved in place, meaning we would decline applications where we could've given them assistance."

"Why though?" Sam asked, "giving hardship helps the arrears index."

"He maintained that the bulk of loans we gave Hardship to fell back into arrears after the assistance period ended. By that time the asset had depreciated further while the loan balance grew. He felt we should repossess them more often, reasoning it was in the client's best interests. But Bree wouldn't have a bar of it, and ended up in HR." There was a loud roar from the patrons as Manchester United scored, sending Ali into a frenzy.

Sam collects the refreshments and makes his way through The Corso throng towards The Burrow where a good crowd has gathered to watch Ronnie perform. As he gets closer he hears a piano introduction and immediately knows Ronnie has Paddy playing in support. Also there is Sherese on percussion and harmonica, and after a few bars comes the distinct dulcet tones of Ronnie as he plays electric guitar.

"I left my heart to the sappers 'round Khe Sanh

And my soul was sold with my cigarettes to the black-market man I've had the Vietnam cold turkey, from the ocean to the silver city And it's only other vets could understand Sam places the Win And Place on the desk in The Burrow as the trio belt out the Cold Chisel classic, which Sam absorbs until the end.

Cold Chisel - Khe Sanh [Official Lyric Video]

"So I worked across the country from end to end

Tried to find a place to settle down, where my mixed-up life could mend I held a job on an oil rig, flying choppers when I could But the nightlife nearly drove me round the bend So I travel 'round the world from year to year And each one made me aimless, one more year the worse for wear And I've been back to South East Asia, but the answer sure ain't there You know I'm drifting north to check things out again Yes, I am, yeah

Chapter 22 Hindsight Review

After returning from New Zealand, Brianna was straight back into the office. Little mention was made of her trip other than to seek assurance she was well, which she surprisingly was. Much better, at least, than when she left.

Also in the Manly office was Renita, deciding she needed to spend more time with the Arrears Management department. As Head of Global Credit, Renita was also in charge of their home loans and credit cards divisions, and car loans rated a distant third in order of importance and profits.

However, she was very conscious that the public would not differentiate: bad publicity for the car loans sector meant bad publicity for Global in general.

After reading the Scholes report for Ronald Jacka, Renita proceeded to review the loan application. While she had confidence in the tight Global lending criteria, Renita wanted to be sure nothing was amiss. And the more she read, the more she knew there was. Ronald Jacka hadn't worked for three years and his income was a veteran affairs disability pension after being diagnosed with PTSD. Initially a Global credit analyst rejected the application but was overruled by a manager after the broker involved complained. Originally, under the assets category, the client had $200 savings and no assets. This was amended to $20,000 in savings and $50,000 in assets, made up entirely of furniture even though the client was renting a one-bedroom unit. There were also no bank statements evident to support the savings claim It occurred to Renita that Ronald Jacka's loan might not be an isolated case, concerned there may be others. As a result she sent an e-mail to Ivan Merchant, the Customer Service Manager, to undertake a review of all loans approved in the last twelve months which have since fallen into arrears.

She laid out a list of particulars to check, including the providing of payslips to verify the income, working longer than twelve months for the same employer, credit score above 650 - all of which are mandatory under Global's lending guidelines - and total assets less than $1,000 when furniture is excluded.

Three hours later, Ivan provided Renita with a list of 148 contracts which met her criteria. Most were initially declined by the analyst but overruled by a manager with common reasons given that credit defaults were paid, income was verified by the broker (but not Global) working less than twelve months for the employer but good employment history, and in almost every case, assets were swelled by the value of their furniture, sometimes as much as $100,000.

Renita raised her concerns with Gavin who reasoned that while they had fallen into arrears at some stage in the last twelve months, they were now all up-to-date, supporting the approval. Renita saw some merit in Gavin's argument but remained uncomfortable, conscious if any of the regulatory bodies were to review these loans, Global could be deemed to be in breach of its lending responsibilities and subject to penalties and fines. They decided to segregate these contracts from the broader Arrears Management and place them with Sensitive Matters. That way, if something did go awry, the client would be dealt with differently.

In room 4.35, Bulldog informed Sam of the development.

"It will be entitled HRG, or Hindsight Review Group" Gavin revealed.

"But 148 contracts?" Sam groaned, "the team is stretched enough as it is."

"On face value it sounds a lot Sam" Gavin said, "but in reality it is a bludge. All the accounts are up to date so they take care of themselves. And if something does go awry, you come to me."

Sam nodded, thinking this would be a good role for Brianna.

"And imagine what this will do for your career" Gavin added, "another feather in your cap."

"Fair enough Bulldog" Sam agreed. "As an aside, did you manage to review the Dorothy Hunt e-mail I sent you?"

"I did," Gavin reacted. "Repossess them Sam" as he rose from his chair while Sam remained seated, "it's a no brainer. I would also treat this as goods at risk as the son is in possession of the assets."

"We don't know that for sure Bulldog," Sam countered, "as I said, we've never actually spoken to the client."

"Of course he's got the assets," Gavin thundered, "what, you think an 86-year-old woman is driving around in a semi-trailer and a tractor? Laughable." as he headed for the door. "I have to get going but this is a good move for you with HRG; your star is definitely on the rise."

"Just one last thing Bulldog" Sam said, "these 148 contracts, are they likely to increase, or is that it."

"Probably increase Sammy" Bulldog responded, "Merchant has been instructed by Renita to review the last five years. I've got another meeting with Renita now but I'll see you later down at The Staines."

Back in the Sensitive Matters domain, Logan is checking the numbers for each SM category, intrigued after being briefed on the Ronald Jacka matter.

"I'm looking at the stats provided by Raj's team and have a guess how many clients we have in Sensitive Matters who suffer from Post Traumatic Stress Disorder. "Logan posed to Mary.

"You mean, how many clients that we know of have PTSD" Mary replied. "I reckon, out of the 1,000 or so accounts in SM, we have about 50."

"Two" Logan revealed, "0.2%. Yet when I looked up what the actual statistics in Australia are, it states it's estimated that 2-20% of all people who have experienced traumatic events develop PTSD and is the second most common form of mental illness."

"Yeah to be honest I have never spoken to anyone saying they suffer from PTSD but, as you well know, I speak to a lot of people with a mental illness, so it's an interesting point you make" Mary responded.

"Just shows you the value in coding these contracts correctly," Logan added, "I wasn't that fussed before but I am now. I want to know how many we have in each sensitive matter category; I guess that is one positive to come out of this debacle."

"I'm still getting my head around it" Mary responded, "I know Collections and mercantile agents are known for their ratbags and cowboys but you'd have thought even they would have baulked at repossessing from a mental facility."

Sam walked in, hearing Mary's comments.

"Ratbags and cowboys, Mary?" Sam remarked, "It wasn't that long ago you were in Collections yourself."

"And now I am in Sensitive Matters," Mary responded, "thank God."

"This Ronald Jacka matter has hit a nerve with the big honchos," Sam advised, "mainly because of the reputational impact on the Global brand. Remember, home loans and super funds dwarf car loans; in the grand scheme of things, we don't really count. My mail is Scholes have done their last repossession for Global."

Brianna arrived back at her desk, "I just wandered past 4.33, I saw Renita talking to Bulldog.

She's normally only in the Manly office if something biggish happens, did I miss anything when I was away?"

"Something big did happen, Bree" Logan replied, "a client suffering PTSD had his vehicle Repossessed."

"Top of the morning Bree" Sam greeted, "great to see you back; how was the trip?"

"It went better than I could've hoped," Brianna replied, "under the circumstances."

"Glad to hear it" Sam reacted. "Once you settle in, I need you to liaise with Johnny Kep re a return of a repossessed vehicle."

Bree looked concerned, "I won't need to speak to the client will I. I know I said the trip went well but what I told you before I left hasn't changed."

"No Bree" Sam instantly responded reassuringly, "I've taken care of it, the only conversation will be with our old mate JK. After that, I have a task for you - managing contracts now coded to Hindsight Review Group, or HRG."

Mary and Logan look up inquisitively at Sam.

"So, team" Sam continued, "I have some more developments. I mean that would hardly surprise you, when is there not something new in Sensitive Matters? After the Veteran's Voice episode

Renita undertook a review of the applications and determined our lending criteria was breached, the loan should never have been approved. They have since uncovered almost 150 contracts in a similar boat and now we have to manage them."

"A hundred and fifty contracts, on my own" Brianna squealed, "nought chance."

"Gosh Sam" Logan sighed, "this Sensitive Matters gig is getting more and more complicated.

As if we haven't already got enough to do and they now hit us with more. The cases we have are already complex as it is, they are all different; it's starting to do my head in."

"Yes they are all different," Mary said, "but they all have one thing in common. They are all trying their best to pay their debt."

"OK everyone," Sam said, "take a deep breath; you are reading this all wrong. Bree won't actually have to do much, very little, in fact. You are making it sound like a much bigger task than what it actually is. The loans in this HRG are all up-to-date. All Bree has to do is keep an eye on them and if one or any of them fall into arrears just let me know. I then inform Bulldog and we work out a plan from there. This way agents won't be engaged systematically."

"Also team," Sam continued, "while you are all here, there is something else I need to tell you.

I'm taking Bree off the phones to do administration and e-mail, a situation I'll review each couple of weeks. VEW Golf will very much still be our model but for now I'm going to give Bree a break from speaking to clients."

Mary and Logan were receptive to the idea, aware Brianna was doing it tough, and as their friend they were concerned for her wellbeing. Mary looked at Sam and wondered if a softening of his hardened stances was beginning to emerge.

"And we keep this one between ourselves," Sam added. As far as everyone else is concerned, you all engage in the same tasks" as he turns to look directly at Brianna.

"Come on Bree, let's go and see our old mate Johnny Kep.

On the other side of the floor, Johnny Kep is sitting at his desk, hard at work, eyes riveted to his computer. But it's not Global work he is undertaking, he is reviewing the photos he took on the weekend, from the Royal National Park in Loftus, south of Sydney.

Sam and Brianna rock up unannounced and both immediately notice the impressive photos on display.

"Wow Johnny boy," Sam greets, "where is that?"

"Royal National Park in Loftus Sam" Johnny replied.

"They are beautiful John" Brianna remarked.

"Australia is a beautiful country" John said, "I could spend a lifetime photographing and still not get halfway around it."

"So why don't you Johnny?" Sam added, "you've got a real talent. you obviously love it too."

"I'm tempted Sam" Johnny reacted, "especially the way the planet is being destroyed at the rate of knots. Beauties that are here today may not be there tomorrow."

"Johnny is big on conservation" Sam said, "we are big on conversation."

The opening bars of the song Kodachrome by Paul Simon start to play. The sound emanates from Johnny's phone.

"This is new, Johnny boy," Sam observed.

"Paul Simon" Johnny informed, "the song is Kodachrome. Apart from the good beat I feel the opening lines pretty well sum me up."

"Before you answer that Johnny," Sam interjected, "Bree is here to help you sort out the car to Ronald Jacka; I'll leave you two in peace."

Sam leaves, and Johnny decides to ignore his phone and talk to Brianna as Kodachrome booms from his mobile.

https://www.youtube.com/watch?v=8rlDTK6QI-w

KODACHROME

When I think back

On all the crap I learned in high school

It's a wonder

I can think at all

And though my lack of education

Hasn't hurt me none

I can read the writing on the wall

Kodachrome

They give us those nice bright colors

They give us the greens of summers

Makes you think all the world's

A sunny day, oh yeah

I got a Nikon camera

I love to photograph

So mama, don't take my Kodachrome away

If you took all the girls I knew

Chapter 23 Best Comeback Since Lazarus

As the week wore on, the dust on the Ronald Jacka matter appeared to have settled and normality resumed with Mary, Logan and Sam at their respective desks while Bree will be arriving later after attending an appointment.

The latest monthly Sensitive Matters report, compiled by Sam, has just been released which an insatiable Mary is digesting. Top of the list is Mental Illness, which covers 58% of all the contracts in the portfolio and is unchanged from the previous month.

One statistic catches Mary's gaze: the jump in numbers for natural disasters, rising from 1% of the Sensitive Matters portfolio to 7%. Mary is aware some parts of Australia have been flood-affected whilst other areas are enduring severe drought. The worst though, is bush fires which have been blazing across parts of Victoria and New South Wales. Mary is also conscious of the fact that, in general, affected vehicles will be replaced at no cost to the client, courtesy of the mandatory insurance when taking out the loan, however after delving deeper into the affected loans themselves, something else has piqued her interest: all the other adversity the client suffers. Losing the car is just one part of the calamity - for many they lose everything.

Disturbed that the bank has no process or programme in place to help these vulnerable clients, Mary conducts a Google search of "banks helping bushfire victims." She quickly hails Sam.

"Sam," Mary exclaimed, "come and have a look at this." Sam was in a good mood. He was reading the latest index figures showing arrears had dropped plus catching up on the latest EPL results.

He was especially chuffed after Everton beat their arch rivals Liverpool and rose from his desk and meandered over to Mary.

"The monthly Sensitive Matters data is out," Mary revealed, "and the figures for natural disasters are through the roof."

"Today is a good day, Mary" Sam responded, "Not only arc the arrears on the way down but Everton beat Liverpool, let me enjoy it."

"Sam" Mary reacted, ignoring his plea, "there are clients of ours whose cars, should I say lives, are going up in smoke, literally."

"Yeah, but the vehicles are insured," Sam reasoned, "and if they can't pay, the Hardship team will extend the loan so they won't have to worry about making payments."

"It's not the car I am worried about. It's everything else" Mary stressed. "Some of our customers are not just losing their car; they are losing everything."

"Well there are plenty of support groups out there to help, not to mention financial counsellors"

Sam countered "after all, that is what they are there for."

"I was thinking we could do more," Mary suggested, "like give them Woolworths or Coles vouchers to buy basic essentials and-"

"Not a chance," Sam snapped, "that is not our role. We already do plenty to help vulnerable clients but that is going too far. We may be charitable but we are not a charity."

"Will Global go broke if she doesn't pay her loan?" Mary asked defiantly.

"Of course not Mary" Sam responded, "but that is hardly the point."

"What is the point, you tell me" Mary said, "I think we should waive all vulnerable customers'

debts" bringing a look of disbelief from Sam.

"You started off wanting a couple of food vouchers and ended up wanting a full debt waiver"

Sam reacted, "talk about going from one extreme to the other."

Mary's reaction was out of frustration, though it inadvertently paved a smoother way to her proposal to provide their sensitive clients with grocery vouchers which, in her mind, would be more palatable to management than a full debt waiver.

"The Constitutional Bank" Mary asserted, "our biggest competitor, I might add, is giving their clients who are victims of the bushfires $400 grocery vouchers."

Sam pulled up a chair and began reading the website. Though he was against the principle, it might sit well with Renita, especially after the Veterans Voice episode with Scholes. This would show Sensitive Matters were genuinely concerned about the Global Car Loans clients' wellbeing. Sam considered Gavin's likely reaction and he knew he wouldn't agree. The thought crossed his mind that he would need to speak to Renita directly.

They are interrupted by Gavin who makes a surprise appearance and is grinning from ear to ear. Ignoring Mary, Gavin talks directly to Sam "Best comeback since Lazarus" he beamed, "what did I tell you Sam, all it would take to get the index back to what we want was a slight tweak in how you and your team do things."

"I agree it's good news, Bulldog" Sam said, "but one swallow does not a summer make; we have to keep this momentum going."

"And that now all the difficult contracts come to us, it's allowed Late Arrears to be even more aggressive than they were before," Mary interjected.

"That too," Gavin replied.

"The customer's not vulnerable" Mary said sarcastically, "now we go super-duper hard with the cash or keys philosophy. Great strategy," she said mockingly.

"Vulnerable or not," Bulldog remarked, "they signed up to pay the loan. They are obliged to pay."

"Even if it kills them," Mary uttered.

Gavin raised his eyebrows at Mary's comments but didn't respond. He motioned to Sam to join him as he walked towards the door. "What's got her goat?" Gavin asked Sam.

"You know Mary Bulldog, always concerned for the customer."

"I doubt she'll be too concerned if she loses her job," Gavin responded, "can't have anyone being anti our collections crew; we are one team, as you know. I have some more interesting, possibly even good, news" as he changed the subject, "I received a notification that Bree applied for a role which is going in Reviews and Investigations, did you know about that?"

The perplexed look on Sam's face indicated this was the first he had heard of it but, in fact, he notified Bree of the role after actively searching the company's job site, Careers Corner, for something solely with her in mind.

After assigning Bree to an administrative role, a decision of which he deliberately neglected to inform Bulldog, he accepted her days at Sensitive Matters were numbered, so set about helping her to find a new job. As Sam and Bulldog conversed, Bree was in a meeting room, two floors below, being interviewed for the position.

"Oh wow," Sam reacted, "that is interesting. Do you think she is a hope?"

"A big hope," Bulldog replied, "I've even contacted Recruitment and put in a good word for her. That investigations team is full of bludgers, so she'll fit right in. This will also fix your headache about her not talking to debtors."

Logan walks past and notices the cologne being worn by Bulldog.

"Hey Bulldog" Logan greets, "you smell nice" as he walks by, bringing an awkward smile from Bulldog.

"What's going on with your team Sam" Bulldog griped, "first Mary bagging her own teammates and now Logan telling me I smell nice. Guys don't say that to guys."

Johnny Kep is seen at the doorway which Sam knows is a sign he wants to speak to him but without Bulldog knowing. However Gavin's sharp eye thwarts that idea.

"Johnny Kep" Gavin yells, beckoning him over to which Johnny obliges.

"What a great month for repossessions," Gavin continues as Johnny joins them, "outstanding effort from you."

"I can't take any credit Bulldog" Johnny humbly responds, "I just get the vehicles ready for auction, it's the Collections guys who do the hard yards."

"Well I'm off to The Staines for a few meetings," Bulldog said, "later on, come and join me.

Sam will already be there, my shout."

"Thanks for the offer Bulldog," Johnny replied, "but as you know, I don't drink or take drugs, I'm a bit of an outlier at this place," as he headed towards the door on his way to his desk. Sam knew he would have to drop in as something was on Johnny's mind.

"Outlier" Bulldog blurted, "what is he inferring with that? I know he doesn't drink alcohol, but he tackles the zero percenters from time to time. Today, I am in a chipper mood, thanks to the index, and I come down here and the place is full of grumps. It's a day to celebrate Sam. See you down there" as Bulldog walks off in the direction of the lifts en route to The Staines.

Sam nods and then receives a text message from Abbey. It's a lengthy piece in which Abbey makes a plea, or more accurately, a demand, they revert to the previous caring arrangements for Vincent where Sam looks after him every second weekend. Sam's preference to discuss matters rather than communicate via text, compels him to call her.

"Hey Abbey," Sam greeted in a welcoming tone, "I got your text. I'm not averse to the idea.

What are you doing, say next Wednesday, I thought we could catch up for a coffee and a chinwag about it."

Abbey explained that she would be with Mark that evening. They were having dinner together, but would be open to seeing him the following night.

"Oh" Sam reacted. "Are you guys seeing each other?"

"Mark is my boss Sam; he is taking me to dinner as a thank you for what he describes as the excellent work I do, which is incredibly and typically generous-hearted of him." After a pause, Abbey continues.

"Mark is also gay, Sam; he and his husband have been married for fifteen years."

"I knew that" Sam responded, "that he was married, but I didn't know it was to a guy, isn't his partner's name Alex?"

"Yes" Abbey snapped, "there are plenty of men named Alex. I don't know what you have against Mark, he is an amazing man - and some might say he is prepared to do more for me than the father of our child.

"I'm sorry, Abbey, I didn't mean to come across the wrong way. I have nothing against Mark"

Sam said apologetically, "just the opposite, I admire the man."

"Thursday then?" Abbey posed.

Perfect" Sam replied, "I'll pick you up at 6."

"How about we meet at the TAB" Abbey countered.

"Gee whiz" Sam reacted, "you haven't been there since Big Ben was a wristwatch. Good Suggestion."

As Sam hung up the phone he overheard Mary talking to a vulnerable client who was complaining after an application for hardship was declined. Mary agreed with the customer and commented that the hardship team can be draconian at times while also criticising the collections team for threatening repossession. When the call ended, Sam told Mary to log out of the system and led her to a jump-in, jump-out room.

"I admire your compassion and commitment Mary," Sam said, "nobody thinks more highly of you than me, but we work for a company, we are one team, and it is not on to bad-mouth your teammates, especially to a client. That reflects poorly on Global and poorly on you."

Mary sat there digesting the feedback and knew she had overstepped the mark.

"I'm sorry, Sam" Mary replied, "I know sometimes I need to take a deep breath and a step

Back."

"If you're having a tough day," Sam explained, "and you want to vent, pull me aside and vent all you like to me. Throw whatever you want at me."

Mary smiled. "I do that anyway Sam, though there is something I want to discuss with you that doesn't concern Sensitive Matters."

Sam looks intrigued.

"There is a role in Diversity, Equity and Inclusion going," Mary added, "I'm looking to apply for it."

"And there is no better person for the job than you Mary" Sam reacted, "that is wonderful news, the job you have always wanted. Of course I will give you the most glowing reference. Let's leave Logan to man the fort and we can grab a daily double and catch the latest at The Burrow. Bree will have finished her interview by now I suspect too."

Sam and Mary leave the office together and head to the TAB. After receiving their daily doubles they drop by the Burrow to be entertained as they eat. Ronnie is strumming his guitar, playing a few chords while Paddy stands up before his piano with his fingers on the ivories preparing to join him. Behind them is Sherese sitting before her drum kit while Ti sits on the ground holding his didgeridoo. Sam gives them a wave which they all acknowledge with a nod of the head, Paddy also smiles.

"Right guys" Paddy says to Ronnie, Sherese and Ti, "it's time."

'YTB" Sherese yells, "Yeah The Buskers." As she gives a quick blow from her trumpet, alerting the onlookers and passers-by that something is about to happen.

"YTB" Paddy adds, "Yeah The Burrow," as Ronnie launches into a guitar intro before being joined by Paddy on piano and Ti on the drums as Sherese stands armed with her trumpet, ready to play later in the piece.

After Paddy mentioned to Ronnie that Sam had a five-year-old son, whom he hardly ever saw, Ronnie suggested they all perform something as a bit of a tribute, saying he not only wanted to choose the song but be the lead vocalist.

Seconds later, the buskers launch into Harry Chapin's "Cats In the Cradle."

https://www.youtube.com/watch?v=KUwjNBjqR-c&list=RDMMkuuSlHw2Dw8&index=3

As the band plays Sam wanders over to Ronnie's Akubra hat, sitting on the ground in front of the performers. Inside are numerous coins and monetary notes. Sam reaches into his wallet and pulls out a $50 bill before placing it in the hat and rejoining Mary.

Chapter 24 Chantelle Khouri

The Sensitive Matters inbox receives, on average, 25 e-mails per day. This is on top of the 20 or so inbound calls they take and apart from them all involving vulnerable clients, they have one major thing in common: they are protracted and complex.

Mary loves the inbox. It's a running joke among the Collections team that Mary is so eager to see what comes in, she reads an e-mail before it arrives. Mary likes to find challenging and complex cases and, during her lunch hour is at her desk browsing through the 37 e-mails to be addressed. One in particular catches her attention; it's from a Jenny Byrne.

"To whom it May Concern

I am a Specialist Family Violence Advocate working in the case management team at Justice Community Legal Centre (JCLC), which is a specialist family violence service in Melbourne's eastern metropolitan region, empowering women and children who are responding to family violence. We provide integrated support, information, case management, safety planning, community education, programmes for pet safety, and a strong network of referral pathways to other services.

Our focus is supporting the safety of women and children and the accountability of perpetrators. JCLC believes in the fundamental human right for women and children to live free from violence and is a child-focused and child-safe organisation.

I can confirm that we are providing case management support for Chantelle Khouri, who has a car loan with your company."

At this point, Mary was almost half-way through the missive. She clicked on another screen to bring up the contract, which she quickly noticed was not coded to SM, this e-mail was the first Global was made aware of the client's plight. The contract was also eight months in arrears and presently with Scholes mercantile agents with instructions to repossess the vehicle. Mary's focus returned to the e-mail.

"...... I can also confirm that Chantelle has been receiving support from us since an assessment was conducted on 6 January. Chantelle is the mother of three children, aged 4,6, and 10, who are all in her sole care. The Common Risk Assessment Framework

(CRAF) indicated that Chantelle and her children were at elevated risk due to the family violence they experienced during a four-year period in their relationship with the perpetrator. Chantelle reported experiencing significant physical, emotional, and financial abuse before fleeing with her three children earlier this year and is now attempting to re-build the life of her and her children."

Mary took another look at the contract. Prior to falling into arrears, Chantelle had maintained a perfect payment history: 3 years and 36 monthly payments, all paid on time. Couldn't it have occurred to someone in Late Arrears that something drastic must've happened to the client to suddenly change?.

Her attention reverted to the e-mail.

"Our client and her children continue to be affected by family violence perpetrated by our client's former partner. Child Protection are involved out of concern for the children should the former partner make contact. Our client and her children have been directed by Child Protection, it is not safe for them to live in any address known to our client's former partner, or in Melbourne's western suburbs generally. An interim

Family Violence Intervention Order obtained by Child Protection in the Children's Court of Victoria are both currently in place to protect our client and her children from our client's former partner. Our client and her children have been living in hotels arranged by the family violence organisation, Safe Steps. She does not have a permanent address and is unable to rent a property unless it is approved by Child Protection.

'The youngest child has a disability and is NDIS supported. The oldest child has severe mental health problems as a result of family violence. Our client cares full-time for her children and is unable to work. Our client's sole income is a Centrelink benefit. The vehicle financed by The Bank is our client's only possession of value. She currently has most of the family's clothes, shoes, and records stored in it. She does this out of fear the ex-husband will find her and the children, and she will need to flee at short notice. Two weeks ago public housing became available but was declined by Child Protection due to safety concerns.........'

Mary approached Sam and discussed the contents of the e-mail.

"Their proposal, after conducting a very detailed assessment and Statement of Financial Position is to pay $40 per week," Mary said as Sam listened while reading the letter from Justice Community Legal Centre

"Justice Legal is amazing," Mary continued. "Aside from dealing with this car loan, they assisted Chantelle with family law, child protection and a range of other issues – and they didn't charge for their services."

Sam was sceptical, "$40 a week for a balance of 22 grand, that would take at least 9 years to pay off, way too long for a car loan."

"This is not a car loan Sam" Mary said, "this is a home loan because that car is Chantelle and her three children's home. All things considered, I think we should waive the debt, the $40 a week is far better with her and her 3 children than with us."

"What is the vehicle worth?" Sam asked.

"About twenty thousand," Mary responded.

Sam considers the suggestion. "OK, so we have a balance of $22k," Sam mused, "after the auction costs are deducted, we'd probably get $18k, leaving about four thousand, ooh...."

"I meant we waive the debt" Mary interjected, "and let her keep the car."

"What!" Sam bellowed, "like smoke. The only time we ever waive a debt is after we have collected and sold the vehicle with the sales proceeds credited to the loan. There is nought chance we will waive a debt AND let them keep the car. I don't even think Bulldog would go for waiving four grand."

"You have just seen what this poor lady is going through," Mary implored Sam sat down to read Chantelle's file. Payments were being made late, often less than what was due and The Bank's efforts to contact Chantelle were unsuccessful. It reached the point where a Notice Of Demand (NOD) was issued. The NOD was not satisfied, and mercantile agents were engaged to repossess the car.

The following day the Late Arrears team received a call from a very apologetic Chantelle. At her side was her husband who, though not a borrower on the contract, wished to discuss the situation with us. As we all know it is not uncommon for a third party to act on behalf of a client, and in this case Chantelle gave her authority for her husband to discuss the matter. He explained they had incurred some unforeseen expenses but would be able to arrest the arrears over the ensuing three months and duly sought a payment arrangement to accommodate this, to which Collections acceded.

Initially, everything looked to be going to plan. The first three fortnightly payments were made by the scheduled dates. But the fourth instalment was not. Neither were the fifth and sixth payments.

The Bank tried to make contact over the phone, but after numerous, fruitless attempts, another NOD

was issued.

A few days later, we received a call from Chantelle again wanting to hand over the phone. But not, as previously, to her husband but to a lady by the name of Jenny who represented the Justice Community Legal Centre. Jenny was a lawyer who worked for this not-for-profit entity which provided free legal services to vulnerable and disadvantaged people.

"The youngest child has a disability and is NDIS-supported. The oldest child has severe mental health problems as a result of family violence. Our client cares full-time for her children and is unable to work. Our client's sole income is a Centrelink benefit. The vehicle financed by The Bank is our client's only possession of value. She currently has most of the family's clothes, shoes, and records stored in it." Jenny advised.

After reading this, Sam became more receptive to Mary's desperate plea and compelling case to waive the debt.

"I'll tell you what Mary" Sam proposed, "I have a meeting with Bulldog in an hour where I aimed to present the bush fire/financial abuse case but will show this to Bulldog instead. If he agrees, you will get your wish."

"He won't agree" Mary blurted, "he's just as hard-nosed as you. He has no heart, Sam. Most people are like Bulldog; he is a walking cliche. They think people should pay their debts, regardless of their circumstances. Why should they be treated differently? I pay all my bills; they should pay theirs is their defiant argument. But every now and again an opportunity comes along for somebody to challenge the status quo

- to help the people in life who can't help themselves. And on this occasion, that somebody is you."

Mary was visibly livid and Sam knew it. He'd never witnessed her in this type of mood before.

"All right," Sam conceded, "I can't make a decision without running it by Bulldog first but you can join me; you can plead the case yourself."

While this scenario wasn't ideal for Mary, she knew this was probably her best opportunity and her high level of self-belief would hold her in good stead with Gavin.

"All right," Mary agreed, "it's not perfect, but I believe I can convince Bulldog."

"With your compelling case" Sam replied, "and conviction, I am certain he will say yes. And I am not 'hard-nosed' while Bulldog does have a heart, I just think his competitive nature gets the better of him sometimes. Let's take five and grab a Win and Place from the TAB before it starts."

"You have the Win Sam" Mary reacted, "I'll have the Place."

As they left the Global office and strode onto the Corso, Sam and Mary could see and hear a new act performing in The Burrow. Paddy was always keen for other musicians to share the stage and be given an opportunity to gain exposure so introduced an "All Comers Day" where once a week, new acts would be allotted an hour to display their talents.

As they approached The Burrow, Sam and Mary observed two elderly, bespectacled gentlemen, impeccably dressed in suits, each wearing a bow tie, were performing a jazz piece. One chap was playing the saxophone while the other was strumming an instrument not seen at The Burrow before - an upright bass. Paddy was supporting them on piano and together they performed Dave Brubeck's Take Five.

https://www.youtube.com/watch?v=vmDDOFXSgAs

Chapter 25 We're A Club, Remember

"You make two very compelling cases, Mary" Gavin said complimentarily, "very hard to say no to that" as he sat next to Stuart and Eric in room 4.38, with Sam standing in the background, after listening to Mary for the previous fifteen minutes demonstrate the reasons Global should waive the remaining debt for Chantelle Khouri.

"Those debtors," Gavin continued, "should be indebted to you" an intended play on words which brought an obligatory chuckle from Eric but no reaction from Sam.

Mary grinned broadly, positively beaming as she looked at Sam before returning her gaze to Bulldog. "So you agree then, Gavin, we should waive the debt" Mary said.

"Of course not Mary" Gavin responded, "what the hell are you thinking, the debtor still has the car remember and we don't waive debts when the asset remains with the debtor." Mary's face turned cold. "But what we can do," Gavin continued, "is to freeze interest, agree to the $40 per week, to be reviewed every two months, and, importantly, allow her to keep the car."

Stuart could see the disappointment in Mary's face, Sam saw it as devastation, Gavin didn't notice anything because he didn't care. Mary thought about challenging Gavin's decision but knew it was a lost cause. She had already made her most persuasive case and didn't have anything to add.

Mary resigned herself to believing any plea she made would fall on deaf ears.

"You know" Mary said with a tinge of despondency, "people do want to pay their debts. But sometimes they just can't. Chantelle has nothing, didn't ask for a debt waiver, offered to pay us $40 per week. An amazing woman" as she politely left the room

"What's your next case Sam?" Gavin asked to which Sam replied there weren't any which wasn't true but he was more concerned about Mary.

"Good" Gavin expressed, "I love it when these meetings finish early, let's have a get-together at The Staines."

They all rise from their seats and prepare to leave with Gavin leading the way. But just as he reaches the door he stops and turns to Sam, indicating what he has to say is an afterthought but, in truth, it has been at the forefront of his mind.

"Oh, that reminds me," Gavin said, "I almost forgot. "Sam, what's this I hear about you going to Renita for some grocery vouchers to give to some debtors?" Gavin asked.

"It was Mary's idea, actually, Bulldog?" Sam responded, "she deserves the credit."

"I'm not worried about that" Gavin said, "I'm talking about going to Renita without coming to me first."

"It's not like you to go rogue," Stuart interjected.

Sam could see how it looked on the surface. Being part of the club meant that Bulldog needed to know everything before anyone else which obviously didn't happen here. However it wasn't a deliberate betrayal of the club, it had more to do with Sam believing he had a better chance of success if he were to bypass Bulldog.

"Definitely not Stuart" Sam asserted, "you know that is not me. Look, I just didn't think of it Bulldog. I have been flat out like a lizard drinking and when Mary wants something she doesn't let up.

It was a simple oversight; it won't happen again."

"The easiest way to ensure it doesn't happen again Sam" Gavin advised, "is whenever you think of anything, your very next thought is the club. You must keep the club members informed."

Gavin gives Sam a reassuring pat on the back and lets him leave the room first. He then glances at Stuart who knows what he is thinking. They may need to keep an eye on Sam.

Logan was utilising the stand-up option of his desk, looking like an orator at a lectern preparing to give a speech whilst eagerly awaiting the outcomes of the presentations, when a disconsolate Mary ambled to her desk.

"No go?" Logan posed.

"I should've known it was a lost cause" Mary said dejectedly, "this was all a charade. A tick the box exercise. Chantelle Khouri never had a chance."

"Not true Mary" Logan asserted, "Chantelle certainly had a chance. Plus these are good experiences for you. As the old adage goes, you learn more from a game you lose than a game you win."

Mary considered Logan's advice which helped to moderate her dejection.

"And" Logan added, "this will be a great experience for when you have the DEI interview."

At The Staines the mood is subdued. Sam is thinking of how Mary is taking the rejection while Gavin is thinking about Sam approaching Renita without telling him first. He wants to give Sam the benefit of the doubt but can't stop thinking it was a rogue act and a breach of The Club's protocol.

Stuart approaches carrying three schooners.

"Tell Sam about how you hoodwinked Renita into keeping Scholes Bulldog" Stuart said excitedly.

This brought a smile to Gavin's face who immediately began yabbering about the case he made to retain Scholes and despite Renita continuing to oppose, he knew her busy schedule would consign this issue into the too-hard basket.

After polishing off a schooner, Sam returned to the office and joined his team. He immediately headed straight to Mary to discuss her presentation and how she felt about it, even though he already had a good idea. As he approached, Mary went from a blank stare at her computer to a steely eyed glare at Sam.

"Why was he so belittling Sam" Mary opined, "I mean I get he didn't agree with me but why did he have to make me feel so small. Especially after he told me I made a 'compelling case' and gave the impression he agreed with me, giving me great hope and self-belief, only to tear me to shreds in the next breath."

"Ah look" Sam sighed, "that's just Bulldog, he's not the only one who is like it and I don't even know if he does it intentionally but sometimes people use it as a tactic: build you up then tear you down so you lose confidence in yourself and back off."

"It worked" Mary conceded, "I know what to say after that."

"But at the same time" Sam said consolingly, "this was a great experience for you, something you can learn from. Next time something like that happens, you will be emboldened. What have I always said to you Mary, BIY, believe in yourself. Believe in yourself as much as I do in you.

Always buy …….. Into BIY."

"Well BIY (as in bye) to you both" Logan quipped, "but firstly Sam I want you to take a look at the contract for Jack Kennedy who passed away recently. Late Arrears have instructed agents to repossess the vehicle."

"Which is the standard procedure" Sam reacted, "unless a third party pays out the loan, you are about to give me a reason why that shouldn't happen on this occasion."

"Jack Kennedy took out the loan" Logan explained, "as a present for his wife Gloria. She was the sole driver and user of the car. In her eyes she owns it."

"She doesn't" Sam said, "as we all know it belongs to Global until it's paid out, something I gather she cannot do?"

"As you would say Sam," Logan responded, "she doesn't have a brass razoo. She is also not working, as her husband was the sole income earner for the household, in which there are two kids by the way and is very reliant on her car."

"Do you have the contract details up on your screen?" Sam asked, sighing, knowing he was faced with another conundrum, requiring in-depth analysis with near-impossible solutions, at least solutions which were amenable to Bulldog.

"Not now sorry Sam" Logan answered as he packed up his laptop, put it in his briefcase and walked to the umbrella stand from where he plucked his surfboard.

"See you tomorrow team" Logan said as he headed to the door carrying his briefcase in one arm and the surfboard under the other.

Sam looked at the clock on the wall to see 3.01 and looked inquisitively at Logan.

"I started early and worked through lunch, remember Sam?" Logan said. It then dawned on Sam that he had agreed to Logan leaving early after weather forecasts indicated the afternoon would bring large, billowing waves to Manly, something Logan was keen to tackle. The blustery conditions led to the beach being closed earlier in the day but that didn't stop Logan, and a number of his fellow surfing zealots from getting out among the waves.

"How could I forget?" Sam acknowledged, "I'll drop by The Staines a bit later and peer out to see how you and your fellow surfbucklers are going, it should be quite a spectacle. Oh, just one thing guys" as Sam scrambles for the television remote and changes the coverage on the screen above from the cricket test between Australia and New Zealand to YouTube.

"Who knows this song" Sam asked

"Dominic Fike" Logan responds instantly, Three Nights, it's a classic as both he and Mary look puzzledly at Sam.

As Logan leaves, Mary's concern has turned to how they will respond to Chantelle Khouri, conscious that Bulldog's proposal is only temporary and in two months when a review is conducted he will look for a way to terminate the agreement and repossess the car.

"So" Mary posed, "I'll ring Justice Community and tell them we'll accept the offer of $40 per week but it will be reviewed every two months."

"Hold off on that for the moment Mary" Sam replied, "I have a plan B."

Over at The Staines, Bulldog, Stuart and Eric have been compelled to leave their favourite haunt, the garden bar, after the blustery conditions forced its closure. They found a vacant table in the corner which was metres away from the hotel's jukebox from which the sound of AC DC's Highway

To Hell is coming to an end.

"Thank God for that" Eric said, "what a racket that was."

"That's a great song Eric" Bulldog countered, "an Aussie classic."

Stuart notices a familiar face as he peers towards the Manly sand.

"What's he doing out here at this time?" Stuart observed. "Bit late for a lunch break."

The others look over and see Logan walking out to the surf carrying his board and wearing a wetsuit, though it's not zipped up with the upper half draped around his lower body, revealing his taut and muscular upper frame and array of tattoos.

"I hope he knows that the beach is closed," Eric added.

"That doesn't stop surfers," Bulldog added, "they love it when the beach is closed, gives them better waves."

Logan's love of the ocean is comparable with his love of being healthy. Apart from his regular surfing stints he works out at the Manly Fitness Fanatics gym at least four times a week, including a yoga session.

"I didn't realise Logan had tattoos" Eric observed.

"Nor me" Stuart said, "maybe that's why he wears a suit every day, to cover them up."

He sure does love his suits" Eric reacted, "wet for the ocean, dry for the office."

Sam makes his way back to The Staines, copping the heavy showers along the way. His aversion to wearing raincoats or carrying an umbrella ensured he was dripping wet when he joined Bulldog, Stuart, and Eric.

"Mate" Bulldog remarked, "this loathing of umbrellas is becoming a sickness. Logan's drier than you, and he's in the middle of the ocean."

"As Johnny Kep would say," Sam responded, "I am just enjoying nature."

As Sam brushed the water off his face and clothes, he peered out at the ocean to catch a glimpse of Logan in the distance, one of about twenty wetsuit-clad surfers braving the tempestuous conditions.

Sam watched Logan catch a wave and he looked to be rocketing along until he lost his balance and came crashing down. Sam then wandered over to the jukebox, put in his bankcard to pay for a song, and selected A38 "The Ocean" by Oxygene https://www.youtube.com/watch?v=aI3yNckfSvU

Chapter 26 Delegations

The following morning Sam arrived at 8.45 to an empty Sensitive Matters domain. Not only was he later than usual, so too were Mary and Logan. Conscious that Mary's unsuccessful bid to convince Bulldog to waive Chantelle Khouri's debt may have weighed on her mentally he was about to ring her when she walked in the door.

"Sorry I'm late Sam," Mary said, "trains were a nightmare."

"How are you feeling?" Sam asked.

"Good," Mary replied, "yeah, good. I'm still a bit peeved over Bulldog's rejection but I'll get over it as you said, "BIY" as she removed her laptop from her bag and placed it on her desk.

"I can't help thinking" Mary continued, "that meeting with Bulldog could've been avoided.

You have the delegation levels, as manager to waive debts. You do not need somebody else's approval."

Sam knew Mary was right and had been considering this for a few days but hadn't mentioned it to anyone. As manager he had the authority to waive debts up to

$30,000, without the requirement to obtain another person's approval. He also knew that if he went down this path, there would be no going back - or up, the corporate ladder - he would be ostracised from "The Club" for "going rogue".

And there were a number of willing candidates ready to take his place.

"I want you to do me a favour." Sam said, "Put together a list of contracts which have loan balances under $30,000 where you feel there is merit in waiving the debt. Any chance you can compile it for me by the end of the week?"

"I'll have it for you by the end of the day" a perplexed Mary affirmed, sensing there may be some hope yet as she donned her headphones to take the first call of the day. "I have a feeling this could be a GLAM."

A sheepish Logan shuffles in the door, self-conscious of his late arrival.

"Sorry I am late guys" Logan said as he plonked his bag on his desk.

"Trains causing havoc?" Sam posed.

"No" Logan replied, "I slept in."

Sam's focus returned to his laptop where he had been reviewing a list of twenty contracts, which, according to Stuart, had loan balances lower than the value of the asset The objective was to convince the client to surrender the vehicle for sale at auction and to reap the surplus funds to buy another vehicle.

Sam's review revealed they all shared a similar theme - the prospective surplus funds would be less than a thousand dollars, barely enough to buy a bicycle let alone a car.

Outside the building, midway between the Staines and The Burrow, Gavin is on his phone, strategically placed so Paddy, who is performing, is out of earshot.

"It might seem minor Stu" Gavin said, "or an oversight as you put it, but any time when someone does something outside the club you have to be careful. I think the world of Sam, you know that, but just keep an eye on him. Maybe this sensitive caper is getting to him."

Paddy wraps up his stint and notices Sam heading towards him believing he is making his way to the TAB.

"Grab me a daily double will you Sammy" Paddy yells.

Sam walks to the Burrow and gives Paddy a hug, "I'm not going to the TAB Paddy" Sam said, "I thought I'd come and see you for a bit of a chinwag but I'm happy to get you a DD if you want."

"Nah mate," Paddy replied, "it's all right. I plan on grabbing a trifecta after Ronnie and Sherese get here, they'll be performing together."

A few seconds later Ronnie, carrying his guitar case in one hand and a cappuccino in the other, and Sherese, armed with a saxophone, arrive at The Burrow. Sherese smiles at Sam and Paddy before sitting herself behind the drum set to prepare for her gig. Ronnie tips his hat and says "how are you me ol chinas," before leaning his guitar against the wall.

"Let's give them a bit of peace" Paddy said to Ronnie, "and we can have that chinwag over a daily double and trifecta."

Sam nods, and they head towards the TAB as Sherese practises the drums, and Ronnie gazes out to the ocean, admiring the twenty-odd surfers, in the thick of the waves.

Sam and Paddy have found themselves a table at the TAB as they wait for their orders.

"So you caught up again with the missus" Paddy said, "this is becoming a bit of a regular Occurrence."

"Hardly Paddy" Sam reacted, "though I must admit it was a pleasant and enjoyable exchange.

You know Paddy, and keep this to yourself, and apologies for changing the subject but in the whole time I have been at Global, both in Collections and Sensitive Matters, we have never waived a debt."

"There's a first time for anything" Pat reasoned, "and from what you just told me, this is the perfect time for it."

"I reckon you love your job," Sam remarked, appearing to change the subject again but related to his own reflections and questioning of his career path.

"Is that what you call it" Pat replied, "a job. Mate, I get to do what I love most - music. And I get paid pretty well for it. I also get to meet all sorts of people, like yourself, and I mean all sorts.

Strangers one day, friends the next."

"It's like that old saying" Sam said, "choose a job you love and you'll never have to work a day in your life." Sam then pondered his situation, knowing that, at this moment, this adage did not apply to him.

"Life was so much easier before Sensitive Matters" Sam said, "everything was black or white - cash or keys. Now, I barely know if I'm Arthur or Martha."

"You're neither" Paddy responded, "you are Sam Crews. And you have an opportunity to make a big difference to disadvantaged peoples' lives. And you have the perfect team to do it."

Sam's mind was now made up. He looked at Paddy and nodded, feeling a huge weight had been lifted from his shoulders. There was no turning back now.

"I have an idea for my team for which I will need your help," Sam said.

An hour later, Sam had quietly returned to the office and parked himself in one of the jump-in, jump-out rooms, one of the many so called cubicles spread throughout the building which enable one to have some time to work alone and uninterrupted. On his laptop Sam was reading a document entitled "Delegation

Levels" which depicted the levels of authority each employee had when it came to making decisions. Now that he was promoted to a manager, Sam attained a Level 4 status which allowed him to authorise a lot more actions than when he was at the Level 3 status of a team leader.

And there were many: from waiving mercantile agent fees, to approving very long-term payment arrangements and reducing the interest rate to name a few. But the term on which Sam had his sights was "Debt Waivers".

Sam had a good idea what they were but wanted to be certain and when he saw he could write off debts up to $30,000 he nodded his head. Just what the doctor ordered. Sam sat back in his chair and gazed into space, thinking of what lay ahead. If what he had planned were to work, it needed to be executed quickly and precisely.

Sam picked up his mobile phone and rang Johnny, asking him to look after the Sensitive Matters phone lines for twenty minutes, to which he typically, unhesitatingly agreed. As Sam puts his phone in his kick, he hears a tap on the room's door and looks up to find it is Renita.

Hey Renita" Sam greets after opening the door, "just leaving now."

"No, no Sam" Renita reacted, "please stay, I'm not after the room, I wanted to see how you are going. I'll be here in the Manly office for a couple of days and like to use some of the time to touch base with as many people as possible."

Sam closed the door behind him and continued the discussion in the aisle. "Pretty good, the results for Sensitive Collections are improving."

This was the first time Sam had ever referred to his team as Sensitive Collections and it prompted the desired result from Renita.

"You mean Sensitive Matters," Renita said.

"Semantics really Renita" Sam replied, "we are just another arm of collections, we just happen to have sensitive in the title." Sam only wanted to plant the seed of misgiving in Renita's mind and let her ponder rather than stand there answering her likely questions to elaborate.

"But I have to go, sorry, Renita," Sam said, "let's catch up later at The Burrow tomorrow, there is someone there I would love you to meet." Sam left Renita whose pensive stare told him his subtle dig worked and returned to the Sensitive Matters domain where Logan was completing some administrative tasks while Mary was focused on compiling the contract details Sam sought from her earlier.

"Guys," Sam said, "put yourselves in After Call Work."

A call appeared in the queue prompting a response from Logan. "I'll just take this call, Sam," he said.

"Leave it Logan" Sam instructed, "Johnny Kep will handle our calls for the next wee while.

Let's go."

Sam, armed with his laptop, headed to meeting room 4.33 with a slightly baffled Mary and Logan following. Sam placed his laptop on the table and plugged it into the big screen where YouTube appeared.

"You guys do a phenomenal job dealing with the most challenging and emotive cases" Sam said. "Our clients' wellbeing is paramount but so is yours. We're going to take a break. I want you to sit back, close your eyes, dream about whatever you want, take a break and enjoy the music."

On the main screen a picture of sheet music appears with a youngish-looking man from a past era, elegantly dressed in a frilly shirt, red tight-fitting coat and what appeared to be a grey wig. As the team peered at the screen; music began to play. Sam was the first to close his eyes with Mary and Logan following suit as they listened to Mozart's Symphony No 40 in G Minor......

https://www.youtube.com/watch?v=JTc1mDieQI8&t=625s

Chapter 27 Sock, Shoe, Sock, Shoe

It's 7 o'clock on a Friday night and Sam sits back on his armchair on his balcony at home, smelling the roses as he stares out into the heavens. For the first time in a while, Sam is feeling good about his job. His balcony is an invitation for lounging as alongside the armchair is an embroidered and cushioned couch. Usually, when Sam relaxes on the balcony, he will either have a guitar in his hand, playing whatever song comes to mind or look out into the skies, letting his imagination run wild.

But this occasion is different: Sam is appreciating nature for what it is.

A magpie flies in and perches herself on the railing, Sam smiles. His newfound love for nature can probably be attributed to Johnny's influence. Or it could be the effect of the sensitive matters and vulnerable clients which have softened his nature and appreciation of what the world has to offer.

More likely though is it is a combination of the two. It could also be his belated and gradual grasping of the responsibility of being a father.

A knock on the door, prompts Sam to turn as it opens where in bounds Vincent with Abbey in tow. A smiling Sam rises from the couch and holds out his arms for Vincent who happily obliges with a warm embrace.

"What are you doing, Dad?" Vincent asks.

"Spending time with the Martians Vince" Sam replied. "Remember those days Abbey" Sam posed, reflecting fondly bringing a nodding smile from Abbey. "A long time ago, well before you were a twinkling in your mother's eye, "Sam continued, I was up there, on Mars, spending time with the Martians."

Spending time with the Martians is Sam's metaphor for thinking about life. Where his mind goes into space and enables him to fantasise and think of life in general. Sam subscribes to the old adage that most people dream when they are asleep, I like to dream when I am awake.

"What was it like?" Vincent innocently asked.

"Magical," Sam responded. "Free as a bird, not a care in the world and able to think about all the positive things in life."

"Sounds like a great place," Vincent remarked.

"I'll leave you two to spend some quality time with the Martians together" Abbey remarked, as Vincent hugged her before joining his dad who moved to the couch, snuggling up as they both looked out at the night sky. As Abbey approached the door she stopped and turned back toward Sam.

"Oh" Abbey added, "one more thing Sam, I'm thinking of going back to uni full-time but I'll chat to you about that another time" as she smiled at Sam then opened the door and left.

Normally this sort of news would alarm Sam but he couldn't but agree that this was merited.

He then looked at Vincent. "Now keep this to yourself," Sam continued, "because it is extremely confidential, you cannot share it with a soul, but I was, in fact, born on Mars. Many years ago when my Earth mum was pregnant with me, she was sitting in the lounge next to an open window when, out of the blue, a giant spaceship hovered above before dropping some tentacles and plucking Mum from her chair, with me in her womb, and kidnapping her. Next thing Mum knows she is on Mars giving birth to me. It turns out that the Starman, who is the top authority on the planet, wanted an Earthling to be born on Mars and that was how they did it."

"But you live here, Dad," Vincent noted.

"Great point son" Sam responded, "after I lived on Mars for eleven years, the Starman wanted to learn more about Earth, so he instructed me to move back with my original family. The Starman also has the ability to erase and change memories so my parents and siblings have the long-held belief that I lived with them the whole time."

"It's OK Dad," Vincent said, "I won't tell anyone."

Sam smiled, not sure if Vince didn't believe him or thought he was joking, or had simply lost interest.

"And just before you arrived tonight son," Sam said, "I was gazing out into space, thinking about work and, in particular, my team, and it dawned on me: we need more bonding sessions away from the office."

Over at The Staines, Gavin and Stuart, who have been there since 11 o'clock that morning, are into their final beer for the evening. Eric, who was with them from the outset, left two hours earlier and about twenty schooners each later, Gavin and Stuart are about to call it a night. As he polishes off his beer, Gavin's eyes are glued to his phone, reading the list of vehicles to be auctioned by Pymbles the following week when something piques his interest, bringing a stern look to his face, a sight not lost on Stuart.

"What is it, Bulldog?" Stuart asked, "what's there?"

"It's what is not there that's the question, Stu" Bulldog replied. "That car from the deceased estate, it has been removed from next week's Pymbles auction."

"Maybe the loan was paid out," Stuart suggested.

"Nope," Gavin replied, "not a brass razoo has been paid on this loan for eight months, and there are no notes indicating a promise-to-pay is in place."

"Maybe the boys discovered we didn't issue the NOD properly," Stuart offered.

"The debtor is dead Stu" Bulldog stressed, "the car was with his wife who is not on the contract so we treat this as goods at risk, we don't need a NOD."

"Yeah but the client has just passed away" Stuart said, "the wife is probably in a bad way and I cannot imagine she would be looking to sell the car."

"Doesn't matter," Bulldog said, "it gives us a chance to repossess without a Notice Of Demand.

Those opportunities do not come along very often."

Gavin looks further into the list and notices a second vehicle was also withdrawn from the auction.

"And here's another one," Gavin blasted, "Ingrid Pavlich's car has been removed. What the hell is going on? Both withdrawals are in the Sensitive Matters portfolio. First thing Monday, we need to speak to Sam."

The following morning, Sam and Vincent are woken up by the alarm to the tune of Everton's Spirit of The Blues But unlike during the week, when it goes at 5.30 in the morning, on the weekend it plays at 7.30. Sam rises from his bed and wanders over to the other bedroom where Vincent has been sleeping.

"Rise and shine Vince," Sam said, "Three Sisters and The Blue Mountains, here we come."

Vince was already awake, wide-eyed and excited after being told by Sam the previous night he had planned a day trip which would involve a hike through the Blue Mountains, a world-heritage listed national park situated about seventy kilometres west of Sydney and the home of, amongst many other attractions, the famous The Three Sisters. As Vince jumped out of bed and gave his dad a hug, Sam hit him with an early morning poser.

"What is the most important thing you will do today, son?" Sam asked.

"Brush my teeth, Dad," Vincent promptly responded. "And?" Sam added. "Tell Mum I love her." Vincent said. "Good lad," Sam said warmly.

"You know son" Sam said, changing the subject, "why does someone who has the best collections record and a propensity to ruthlessly repossess cars, be charged with managing the contracts of our most vulnerable clients? Is it because I'll keep doing that, and that is exactly what Bulldog wanted all along?"

Vincent looked understandably confused, bringing a smile from Sam, who left the room with Vincent quickly following him. Sam had prepared Vincent's attire for the day, and after changing out of his pyjamas, Vincent perched himself on the couch and proceeded to put on his shoes and socks.

This piqued Sam's interest.

"Aha," Sam said, "so you are a sock, sock, shoe, shoe person."

"Huh?" Vincent reacted.

"You put on both socks first before putting on your shoes," Sam explained, "that makes you a sock, sock, shoe, shoe person."

"What are you, Dad?" Vincent asked.

"Me" Sam Said, "I am a sock, shoe, sock, shoe fella."

"What is the difference?" Vincent asked.

"Apart from being a different format" Sam replied, "I'm not overly sure. But I do the sock, shoe order because I think if I put both socks on first, I may not put on the shoes straight away and walk around in my socks. Could make me become lazy."

"Before we go Dad," Vince said, "can we spend a bit more time mixing with the Martians?"

"Great idea son," Sam said as Vince rose from the couch and headed to its namesake on the balcony. Sam considered grabbing his guitar but opted for Spotify instead and while Vincent sat looking at nature, Sam quickly put together a playlist, with the aim that each song has an inference or connection to nature. As he enters the balcony and joins his son, he is taken by Vincent's deep gaze into the elements.

"What are you looking at son?" Sam asked.

"The trees Dad" Vincent remarked, "I love looking at the trees." At that moment, a bird flies in and rests on the railing.

Sam ponders Vincent's comment and nods approvingly. "You don't know Johnny Kep" Sam said "but he knows a lot about you. He also knows a lot about nature, and I reckon he would love to be here with us right now. I never really appreciated nature like I should've son. I never really appreciated people like I should've."

Vincent looks at Sam before returning his gaze to the trees rooted a few metres away as Sam follows suit, realising this was the first time in the two years he has been living there, that he appreciated their beauty.

As they sit together, enjoying nature, a new tune on Spotify begins, one which is foreign to Sam. The sound of birds tweeting is instantly followed by guitaring before a male's voice emerges:

John Hanlon's "Damn The Dam"

https://www.youtube.com/watch?v=uILC4gk5As

Leaf falls to kiss the image of a mountain

The early morning mist has ceased to play

Birds dancing lightly on the branches by a fountain Of a waterfall which dazzles with its spray Tall and strong and aged, contented and serene The kauri tree surveys this grand domain For miles and miles around him, a sea of rolling green Tomorrow, all this beauty won't remain Damn the dam, cried the fantail.

As he flew into as he flew into the sky

To give power to the people

All this beauty has to die

Chapter 28 Bonding with The Buskers

Monday dawns, heralding not just a new week at Sensitive Matters but also a new sense of vigour. Mary is very upbeat over the prospects of finally giving the assistance the vulnerable clients need, and, in her firm view, deserve, while Bree has just learned she was successful in her bid for the role in Remediations and Investigations, her joy of which is shared by her colleagues. Logan is not just happy for her, he is happy for himself, reasoning that working in Sensitive Matters will open more doors. If you can master this role, you can master anything, he thought.

Mixing with the Martians gave Sam an idea for team bonding, prompting him to quietly nip out to The Burrow where Sherese on keyboards, Ti the didgeridoo and Ronnie singing and playing guitar, were performing their version of The Doobie Brothers' "Long Train Running".

https://www.youtube.com/watch?v=CVsLEI-hCXw

As they performed, Sam quickly approached Paddy who was sitting on his comfy chair tackling the SMH's cryptic crossword for the day.

"Good timing Sam," Paddy replied, "I'm stumped with today's cryptic crossword, this one is eating at me. One word, eight letters: 'Sounds like a good social event to line up for a haircut."

Sam thought about it and five seconds later said, "barbecue."

Paddy digested his answer and mouthed the word slowly to himself, helping him to understand the rationale, "barber queue", before smiling and adding it to the crossword.

"I've come up with a brainwave," Sam said, "and, sure enough, it involves you."

"I gather it requires me to perform in some capacity," Paddy mused.

"Yes" Sam replied, "but not as much as you may think. The main thing is to use The Burrow for about ten or fifteen minutes, at around 4.30, to perform a team song."

"Sure" Paddy said, "what do you have in mind?"

"Dominic Fike?" Sam posed.

"I love Dominic Fike" Paddy intoned, "what are we talking about, 'Babydoll, Phone Numbers-"

"Three Nights," Sam asserted.

"Quite a vocal range that one, Sammy," Paddy said.

"You can sing the high notes," Sam responded.

As Sherese and Ronnie finished playing, to warm applause from the sizeable crowd, Paddy beckoned them.

"Right guys" Paddy said, "a change of plan. We need to rehearse a new song, and it's good that you brought your saxophone today, Sherese."

"Do you mind if I play your guitar Ronnie?" Sam asked.

"Go for your life me ol china' Ronnie replied, prompting Sam to pick up the guitar and start strumming.

"Right team" Sam said, "this is how we are going to play it."

The clock ticked past 3 p.m. and over at The Staines, a crowd of Global employees is assembling, more than twenty of them, most of whom hail from the Credit department. They were there to farewell their colleague and friend Adeel Makhur, who had abruptly resigned and asked to give just one week's notice instead of the obligatory four (weeks). Adeel cited the reason as needing to attend to an ailing relative and while there was some truth to this the main reason was Burton Briggs.

Two weeks prior, Adeel assessed a loan application from Burton Briggs, seeking to purchase a $120,000 Mercedes, and after discovering a credit file containing three defaults and two court judgements, he proceeded to decline it. However, two days later, at the behest of Mark Bryers, who had recently been promoted to a senior manager, that decision was overruled, and the loan was approved. This was the final straw for Adeel. While this wasn't the first of his decisions to be rescinded, he wanted it to be his last and knew the only way this could happen would be to quit.

Back in the office Sam is hastily arranging with Johnny to take SM inbound calls from 4 o'clock to 5 o'clock to enable his team to finish an hour before the scheduled knock-off time. Sam stressed to Johnny the importance and purpose of keeping Gavin in the dark, to which Johnny obliged.

As 4 o'clock approaches, an upbeat Sam returns to the Sensitive Matters fervour, smiling as he walks in to see his team typically hard at work. Bree, who has two days left with the team, is devoting her time to reviewing the latest list of contracts to be assigned to her HRG list, while Logan is feeling very pleased with himself, having just finished a call with one of Scholes' tow-truck operators where he thwarted a vehicle being repossessed.

"You are looking very chuffed," Sam remarked.

"Daniel Casey," Logan smiled.

"Came to us overnight" Sam reacted, "mental illness?"

"I knew you'd know Sam" Logan said, "but I bet you didn't know it was still out with agents for repossession. Customer Service coded it to us after speaking to his financial counsellor, but it was with Late Arrears and they failed to inform them."

I am guessing you rang Scholes to put a halt to it

"Not Scholes." Logan replied, "I rang the towie directly, just got off the phone to him. He was 15 minutes away from Daniel's house."

Mary, who had been listening to the entire conversation, chimed in.

"Great work" Mary said, "we also owe a bit of gratitude to Johnny Kep for giving us the agents' and tow-truck drivers' mobile numbers."

"Did he now" Sam said, "I wasn't aware of that, but it was a smart play. Up here for thinking, down there for dancing."

"HRG list is all in order Sam" Brianna interjected, "who are you planning to manage it when I go in a couple of days."

"Good question Bree Sam responded, "I don't know yet but now I want everyone to wrap things up, we are all heading out for a bonding session."

"I think you'll find The Staines is pretty full," Brianna said, "it's Adeel's last day and his team are farewelling him there."

"Who said we are going there" Sam said "and thanks for the reminder, I forgot it was Adeel's last day. As I said, finalise what you are doing. We are finished for the day and I'll see you all out the front of the office in six minutes."

Sam made a beeline for the stairs and sprinted to the main exit before darting to The Staines, where he greeted Adeel and his colleagues.

"Mate, so sorry you are leaving," Sam said to Adeel as they embraced, "but I can completely understand why. I'll be back to join you for a beer, but before then, I want you and your pals to come to The Burrow."

"Sure Sam" Adeel replied, "when?"

"Four minutes" Sam replied, "see you guys out there."

As Sam dashed to the Burrow, an unexpected visitor arrived at the Staines, Mark Bryers. He quickly approached Adeel.

"Mate I can't stay," Mark said as he shook Adeel's hand, "but I just wanted to thank you for all your efforts at Global and wish you all the best for the future."

Adeel was taken aback, appreciative that Mark would take the time to farewell him and express warm sentiments.

"That's really nice of you Mark' Adeel reacted, "I appreciate it mate."

Mark turned, acknowledged some of Adeel's co-workers and left The Staines and, as he hit the Corso, muttered to himself, "good riddance buddy, let's put someone in there who is an approver, not a rampant decliner like you."

Sam arrived at the Burrow to see Paddy, with his guitar slung over his shoulder, resetting the microphone stand while Ronnie and Sherese waited patiently. Sam mouthed "one minute" to them before returning to the front door of the Global office. Mary was already there while he could see Logan and Brianna trekking towards them. As they arrived Sam said, "Follow me."

As they approach The Burrow they see and hear Paddy performing a guitar solo, the intro for the Dominic Fike song, "Three Nights".

https://www.youtube.com/watch?v=nb6ou_k4OzM

Paddy then starts singing "Bah bah bah bah...."

Within a flash Sam has joined Paddy and sings into the microphone, already set up on its stand.

He takes over the vocals: "Three nights at the motel, under streetlights in the City of Palms. Call me what you want, when you want, if you want. And you can call me names if you call me up."

As Sam sings, he gestures to Logan, Brianna and Mary to join them in The Burrow, which they do, and within seconds, they are all in on the act. Logan knows every word of the song, unlike Brianna and Mary who do their best to sing along.

"Three nights at the motel, under streetlights in the City of Palms. Call me what you want, when you want, if you want. And you can call me names if you call me up.

Sam dons the conductor's hat and points to each person when it's their turn to sing, beginning with Logan.

Logan - Feel like the least of all your problems; you can reach me if you wanna, Stay up tonight, stay up at night.

Sam - Green lights in your body language. Seems like you could use a little company from me.

ALL - But if you got everything

SAM - figured out, like you say

ALL – Don't waste a minute, don't wait a minute

PADDY – It's only a matter of time

ALL - for you to tell me now,

SAM I've been up for

BUSKER I've been up for

ALL - Three nights at the motel

Under streetlights in the City of Palms

Call me what you want, when you want, if you want

And you can call me names if you call me up

SAM - (call me up)

ALL - Three nights at the motel

Under streetlights in the City of Palms (what you want, ay)

Call me what you want, when you want, if you want

And you can call me names if you call me up

They sing the song until its end, with Paddy finishing off with a guitar solo.

Chapter 29 Member Of Parliament

"Who the hell is Claire Neale?" Gavin barked at Stuart and Eric, inside their favourite meeting room, The Staines, taking advantage of Happy Hour, where schooners were half-price from 3.30 until 6.30. They arrived at 3.31.

"She's a federal member of parliament, Bulldog" Eric answered.

"No shit Sherlock" Gavin snapped, flashing his phone at Eric revealing the letter e-mailed by Sam. "It says that on the letterhead. I mean, who the hell is Claire Neale to demand we waive a $22k debt! We already went through this same debtor with a financial counsellor where we gave them a very good offer. Return the vehicle, and we will waive any shortfall."

Bulldog's preference to communicate orally rather than via e-mail or text as, in his eyes, it led to faster outcomes, was overlooked by Sam. After receiving the letter from Griggsy a few weeks earlier, he reviewed the account and concluded the MP was right. Sam figured to get Bulldog on board he should e-mail him first to give a heads-up before they discussed the merits of the request. It backfired, Bulldog didn't need a discussion; his mind was made up.

"I'll grab us four schooners lads," Sam yells as he strolls past them heading towards the bar.

Over In Barangaroo, a very relaxed Abbey is sitting at reception chatting to Mark who is standing alongside her.

"It's the first time I have been to a show of any capacity in a long time Mark," Abbey remarked, "thanks for taking me, it was such a great experience."

"A Chorus Line is great" Mark uttered, "seen it quite a few times.

Many memorable scenes but I think my favourite is the monologue."

"Mine was when they performed "What I Did For Love," Abbey opined "When the voiceover said if today were the day you had to stop dancing, how would you feel? I became emotional It was so impactful. I just sat there gazing at these dancers, in total admiration at how much they loved what they were doing and couldn't bear the thought of not doing it."

"That's what you call dedication and passion," Mark added.

"If today were the day you had to stop being a doctor, Mark" Abbey asked, "how would you feel?"

"I'd feel pretty good," Mark quipped, "No, I don't know, I guess I'd be a bit sad. After all, I help to get a lot of women pregnant."

"Well, last night's show convinced me to take you up on your offer," Abbey said, "I'm going back to uni full-time."

Over in the Sensitive Matters Domain, Logan and Mary are at odds over the likely outcome of the debt waiver request.

"I love your optimism Mary" Logan said, "especially after your experience with Bulldog and Chantelle Khouri. And whilst I agree the debt should be waived, I am fairly certain Bulldog will not have a bar of it."

"Chantelle Khouri would've given Bulldog much food for thought" Mary countered, "I think he'll be softened by it and realise we have a great opportunity to be the best bank in helping vulnerable clients. I am fairly certain Bulldog will agree."

"Like smoke, we are waiving the debt," Bulldog bellowed at Stuart and Eric as he stood with both arms outstretched and hands firmly planted on the table at The Staines, "that MP can go and jump in the tide. And where is Sam with those beers? He is slower than a wet week."

Seconds later, Sam returned from the bar carrying a tray of four schooners, then proceeded to hand one each to Bulldog, Stuart, and Eric before calmly pulling up a chair and, unlike the others who were standing, sat down by their table.

"I have to say Bulldog," Sam said, "and you know we are both two peas in a pod in just about everything, including an aversion to debt waivers, but this MP makes a compelling case. Domestic violence, financial abuse, mental illness, you name it, the client is a smorgasbord of sensitive matters."

"Compelling?' Bulldog responds, "the only thing compelling is the bullshit the MP spouted.

She was carrying on like a two-bob watch."

Sam's temperature is starting to rise. Normally very composed, he takes issue with Bulldog's attitude but is careful not to show his hand. He felt strongly that if there was ever a time when Bulldog would agree to a debt waiver while the client kept the car, it would be now.

"I'm not a believer in waiving a debt either, Bulldog," Sam said diplomatically, "you know that. But apart from all the client's suffering there are two pertinent points here which make this more likely. Firstly, it's addressed to our CEO, and secondly, it's from a federal member of parliament. The backlash would be enormous if we don't do what is asked."

"You don't know that," Bulldog responded, "it's possible the MP didn't even write this, and it came from some lackey in her office. And I can guarantee our CEO did not read this. It may have been addressed to the CEO but he wouldn't read it, not a snowball's chance in hell; he wouldn't even know about it. One of his thirty-seven EA's would've read it and later passed it on to you."

Aware he was losing the argument, Sam had a rush of blood and changed tack, bringing up examples he felt would bolster his causes.

"You realise Late Arrears wrote off 2 Mercedes and a Porsche yesterday because of skips, almost $500k just because they can't find them," Sam said. "At least this client is talking to us."

"Semantics" Bulldog reacted. "And I'm not sure what your point is here. You know as well as I do they were written off from the live book to be pursued by our Loss Recovery team. We did not waive these debts, they are still due and payable."

"If we find them," Sam responded, "probably been shipped to another country by now."

"We'll find them," Bulldog asserted, "and we are getting off-topic here."

Stuart and Eric watched on with interest as Bulldog downed half his schooner in one gulp.

"What we will do, Sam," a calmer Bulldog offered, "is what we said we will do to the financial counsellor who tried a similar thing on us weeks ago, "we can take back the car, sell it, and absolve the client of any liability for the shortfall."

Sam acknowledged Bulldog's decision but now realised he was moving into a different world.

If Bulldog wouldn't agree to waiving this debt, which was as compelling a case as he'd ever encountered, there was no hope any of the loans on the Sensitive Matters portfolio would fit the bill.

And Sam identified at least eight loans where he wanted to waive the debt. It dawned on Sam he was now on his own.

"Well, better get back to this MP and tell her the request is declined," Sam said as he quickly polished off his beer. "See you lads."

As Sam made his way back to the Sensitive Matters domain, he impulsively thought of visiting his old team, an image which brought a smile to his face and lightened his mood. As he approached the Late Arrears area he could tell there was a lot happening but not concerning collections.

"Channing Tatum" Sean Hogan yells at his fellow Late Arrears teammates after putting the client to whom he was speaking on hold to enable him to answer the conundrum. Every now and then, in the final hour of the day, the collections teams like to play a particular game, with each team member taking a turn in choosing the subject of merriment. On this occasion, it was Roy Benz's turn who plumped for "Anagrams of Famous People" which involves Roy shouting out an anagram, and the team have a minute to provide the answer. Forty-eight seconds after Roy revealed "Unmatching Tan".

"Well done Mr Hogan," Roy acknowledged, "that now puts you alone at the top of the leaderboard. The next one is "I Like Me Young".

Mans is also on the phone talking to a mercantile agent who believes the client sold the vehicle to a third party.

"He can't do that mate" Mans reacted, "it's not his car to sell. Do we know who bought it?"

Mans writes down the details provided then hangs up the phone.

"Goods at risk guys" Mans yells. "$30,000 left owing on the loan and the debtor sold the car."

"Do we know to who?" Roy asked.

"Yeah," Mans replied gleefully, "name and address. Agents are heading out there now. The buyer will not only have to hand us back the car, he will lose the $40k he paid the debtor."

"No sympathy" Roy snapped, "he obviously didn't check PPSR."

At that moment, Sam strolled in. "What is this having a session without your favourite team leader?" he blurted as he shook Mans' hand.

"I thought our games gig was beneath you now that you have moved up to the board room level," Roy gibed.

"Once in Sam's team, always in Sam's team," Sam quipped, "you know that guys. So what's the game?"

"It's Anagrams of Famous People" Mans evinced, "currently Sean is winning."

"Well, not for much longer," Sam said confidently as he pulled up a chair, "throw it at me."

"The anagram for the famous person is "I Like Me Young," Roy said. "And you are not allowed to write it down, mental image only."

Sam, like the rest of them, sat in silence, running the anagram through his head before it dawned on him: "Kylie Minogue!" Sam shouted.

"You've still got it, Sam" Mans said admiringly.

At that moment Sam received a text from Mary: "Where are you?" Sam knew she and Logan would be anxiously awaiting the outcome of the meeting so opted to cut his time with his old team short.

"I have to skedaddle folks," Sam said as he glanced over Roy's shoulder at his laptop to see the remaining questions: "REBORN EDITOR Robert De Niro, A NEON SMILE, Liam Neeson.

"I'd have got those Roy," Sam said as he headed back to his desk.

Back at the office, Sam walked into an eagerly awaiting Mary and Logan.

"We're going to do it" Sam said, "Mary, I want you to draft up a letter advising the MP the debt will be waived and the asset is to remain with the client. I need it pronto, so if you can get it back to me by 5 o'clock so I can proofread it and send it to our MP friend by day's end."

"I told you so, Logan," Mary said as he started typing on her computer, beaming a broad smile.

Logan sat there, surprised but impressed. "It's a GLAM."

"Yep" Logan acknowledged, "I am happy to admit when I am wrong."

"We also need to be discreet with this" Sam added, "don't want anyone to know just yet, a very sensitive issue, so please do not tell a soul."

Back in Barangaroo, Abbey is typing an e-mail to a client while speaking on the phone. As she hangs up she switches her laptop to a site she had open before the phone call. It is YouTube where a picture of a line of about twenty people, all in their youth, appears. They are all dancers performing in a musical.

A voice emerges from the still photo:

"If today were the day, you had to stop dancing, how would you feel?"

Abbey smiles as she watches a rendition of "What I Did For Love" from the musical A Chorus Line.

https://www.youtube.com/watch?v=6kg3Z-ZEuYI

Chapter 30 The Plan

The following morning at 7.35, seated at a table in the far corner of the TAB are Logan and Mary, after receiving an invitation from Sam the previous evening at 11.30 for an ad hoc meeting.

Their eyes are fixed on Sam, who sits across from them on the other side of the table, listening intently to him revealing his latest strategy for Sensitive Matters.

Carla approaches carrying a tray bearing a daily double for Sam and a Win and Place each for Logan and Mary. She recognises they are in a serious discussion and politely smiles before placing their respective refreshments in front of each of them without saying a word. Sam concocted a plan to waive debts, explaining the reason he asked Mary to compile a list of loans with balances under $30,000 was because they were within his formal delegation level, ones where he did not need approval from Bulldog.

"Of course," Sam said, "we cannot show our hand. Nobody outside us three and Johnny Kep is to know about this. And when I give you the green light, you will need to be swift."

"It's a great plan, Sam" Logan said, "but I am a bit worried about how this will impact my career progression. I gather my hope for an L3 anytime soon will be dashed."

"Yes Logan, there is that potential component," Sam said, "it's a fair point, and while the onus - and blame - should fall fairly and squarely on me, you guys may incur Bulldog's wrath, talk of going rogue, all that sort of stuff."

"I could not care one iota," Mary reacted, "you have plenty of time for career progression Logan, these vulnerable clients need our help now."

"In fairness Mary" Sam said, "you and Bulldog have never seen eye-to-eye, and you weren't top of his Christmas card list. Logan, on the other hand, has a lot of respect from Bulldog."

"He does?" Logan said astonishedly.

"Absolutely," Sam responded. "You were his first choice for the team. He described you as being "cultured and refined".

Logan chuckled. "You know why that is," he said

"one day I was at The TAB, and while waiting for a trifecta, a horse race was on one of the televisions, so with nothing else on I casually watched it unfold. I'm not into horse racing but I was bored and while watching, I heard the commentator call one of the horses 'Savile Row' which I thought had a bit of a ring to it so later that day, I looked it up on the internet. 'Look it up Logan' he said sarcastically.

"I learned," Logan continued, "that it was a place in London that made expensive suits. So one day Bulldog wore a nice suit and I said to him 'you are looking very 'Savile Row' as a bit of a joke, and he was so impressed. He commented that I obviously have great taste. I wouldn't know a Savile Row suit if I fell over one."

"Well let's just keep that our little secret, shall we?" Sam responded. "And Mary - phenomenal effort to send me those contracts so quickly, your blood is worth bottling – but I thought there would be about eight loans to waive, you sent me twenty-eight."

"Tell me one of those where we shouldn't waive Sam" Mary reasoned. "The truth is all vulnerable people should have their debts waived."

Sam glares at Mary. He is taking a big risk in waiving any of the debts without Bulldog's knowledge and is irked by Mary's lack of understanding.

"You remind me of when I was growing up and I'd ask Dad for $5, and when he said yes, I would go, 'can you make it $10?" Sam reacted.

"But I'll settle with twenty-eight Sam," Mary added with a smile.

"Twenty-eight!" Logan said, initially surprised at the high number, though when reflecting on Mary's diligence, he knew Mary would've made very thorough and rational cases for each. "Actually, when I think about it, that doesn't surprise me."

"I'll review them this morning," Sam said, "so it's not a done deal yet."

"Plus" Logan said, "we have to get real here. There is nought chance that Bulldog will not know of this at some point, quite soon. And when he does, there will be smoke coming out of his ears."

"I agree, Logan, so I have a plan," Sam explained. And it involves two key ingredients:

Sensitive Matters Friday and Renita Bray. At the next SMF, I will present one of our worst cases and, unbeknown to Bulldog, Stuart, and Eric - Renita will be there. I have mentioned Sensitive Matters Friday to her before and she expressed an interest in attending. I will tell Renita then send the invitation at the last minute so Bulldog doesn't get wind of it. I am confident after my presentation

Renita will recommend a debt waiver, which Bulldog will have to accept. That will give us a green light to waive a debt which is warranted, or supported by the facts. After that we get into gear to waive the other twenty seven, or so.

Mary and Logan both nodded approvingly. This was a very positive moment for them, not to mention a relief. But Sam had very mixed feelings. It was a good move for their vulnerable clients - and the right move - but he knew this would spell the end of his career at Global, at least with Bulldog at the helm.

"What we will need to be conscious of, though is time," Sam continued. "Once I present these cases and get Renita's agreement, Bulldog's first thought will be that I could've gone rogue. If he's in two minds at the start of the meeting, he will have no doubt by the end of it. My club membership will be rescinded. So he will pull out all stops to make things hard for me so you two will need to launch straight into waiving the remaining debts.

'I will spend the rest of the night drafting up summaries for each loan, outlining the reasons for the waivers. I will then send them to you via e-mail. Once that Sensitive Matters meeting ends and I give you the signal, you jump straight into closing the accounts and removing the encumbrances from PPSR. The next 24 hours we will be flat out like a lizard drinking."

"Maybe we should tell Eric to add this to Kanban," Logan said sarcastically.

"Or Kanwaive (debts)" Mary quipped.

A feeling of disquiet comes over Mary. While she is ecstatic at the thought of these vulnerable clients getting their debts waived, her joy is tempered over the likely repercussions for Sam.

"On a serious note though, Sam, I guess that means getting a promotion to senior manager is off the table for you." Mary opined.

"That's incidental, Mary" Sam reacted, "whatever happens happens, but I do think this is the right approach, the right thing to do. And this is likely to be our only opportunity to execute this plan.

Our focus is not to be on the consequences for us, it is the consequences for these vulnerable clients.

Let's do this. Let's make every post a winner."

A couple of hundred metres away, Gavin enters the office and takes the lift on his way to his desk, unaware of the gathering at the TAB. While it may be an unusually early start for the Sensitive Matters team, it isn't for Gavin, who is invariably one of the first people to set foot in the Global building. The old adage of "works hard, plays hard" half applies to Bulldog. In his case, he works hard and when appearing to socialise, continues to work hard. The previous day's meeting with Sam is playing on Gavin's mind as he pulls out his phone and rings Stuart, which it goes to voice-mail.

"Mate," Gavin said, "I've been thinking a lot about yesterday's meeting with Sam. I wasn't very happy with how it unfolded. I think maybe I've been a bit hard on the lad and haven't given him enough recognition for the good job he is doing so I'm going to recommend he be given an extra $10,000 when the annual bonuses are set next month. Anyway, we'll discuss it when you get here."

Gavin hangs up and moves to his desk where he opens his laptop and proceeds to prepare for the day ahead.

Later that night, at 10.30, Sam is at his desk in the office, reviewing the submission from Mary.

He knows the cases must be watertight so when he agrees with Mary's proposal, he focuses on writing a very detailed summary, conscious there will be many sets of eyes analysing his reasons.

Sam is also plagued by the large number. He agrees with seventeen of them but feels the others have plausible alternatives to a debt waiver.

After sending Mary and Logan an e-mail with the list of approvals, Sam then casts his attention back to the remaining eleven contracts and asks himself if there really is a credible alternative or he is baulking because of the high number of loans in question.

It also occurred to Sam that other, plausible options have been the norm at Global since he started there; waiving a debt was heresy. Sam sat staring at his laptop, pondering his next move. He looked up at the television screen to see a still photo of Global Home Loans, advertising its 5.95% variable rate before walking to Mary's desk and plucking the remote control, muttering to himself, "I'm going to take a leaf out of Mary's book" and switched the coverage to YouTube then typed in the name of his favourite rap singer.

As Sam walks back to his desk, he looks up at the television to see two young men embrace to the sound of a piano introduction. Sam then sits down and watches Eminem and "Lose Yourself."

https://www.youtube.com/watch?v=_Yhyp-

_hX2s&list=RDMM&start_radio=1&rv=Mx77bIJWDqQ

Chapter 31 Withdrawal Symptoms

The next morning, an emboldened Logan is feeling a box of birds. He arrives at the ferry terminal at 6.10, armed with his surfboard and work-bag, before dropping the latter at his desk and taking the former into Global's changing rooms, where he dons his beloved wetsuit and heads out to the beckoning surf. The waves are a good three metres high but Logan tackles them with aplomb. After an hour in the water, he glides back to shore and scampers to Global's changing rooms, where he quickly showers, swaps his wetsuit for a newly purchased Van Heusen navy blue suit and is at his desk at 8.15.

Sam's plan has given him a new lease on life, prompting a review of his portfolio. There is also Sandie Chan.

Sam had been at his desk since 7.00, preparing for Sensitive Matters Friday and reviewing the last contracts on the list, conscious it will be the first words out of Mary's mouth when she walks through the door.

"I know you have a lot on your plate Sam," Logan said, "I've had this one for a few weeks now and have been meaning to run it by you. The client's name is Sandie Chan, who is a co-borrower with her ex-husband and wants her name taken off the loan, to remove her liability."

"Sandie Chan" Sam reacted, "I don't recall her name on Mary's list."

"That's because it's not a request for a debt waiver," Logan responded, "Sandie is happy for the other borrower to pay, just not herself."

"On what grounds?" Sam asked.

"She claims she was forced to sign as a co-borrower" Logan explained, "as her ex had a bad credit rating and couldn't get the loan on his own. The vehicle is a 4-wheel drive Ford Ranger, which he uses solely for work and weekends away - without her. Sandie not only has no use for the vehicle, she has never even driven it."

Sam listened intently. He knew the Banking Code of Practice (BCOP) contained clauses where there are legitimate grounds for the removal of a guarantor.

"I took your advice, Sam" Logan continued, "I looked it up, Logan" bringing a chuckle from Sam, "and under BCOP, chapter 17 # 56: 'You may end your liability by giving us a written request to do so in the following circumstances: 'Where credit has not been provided or relied upon". It also states that 'If, on the information that you have provided to us in the course of applying for this loan, you will not receive a substantial benefit from the loan, we will not approve you as a co-borrower unless we:

a) have taken reasonable steps to ensure that you understand the risks associated with entering into the loan, and understand the difference between being a co-borrower and a guarantor; b) have taken into account the reasons why you want to be a co-borrower; and c) are satisfied that you are not experiencing financial abuse.'

There is no doubt in my mind, Sam," Logan concludes, "this loan should never have been given in the first place."

"I have to catch up with Johnny Kep," Sam advised "but I'm not disagreeing with you. Let me give it a bit more thought. I take it we received the request from the client in writing?" to which Logan nodded.

Sam was in a hurry to speak to Johnny. Aside from the matter of which debts warranted waiving, there were vehicles in the Sensitive Matters portfolio slated for the upcoming auctions, the next one of which is the following day. With his new mindset, Sam reasoned these cars may not have been repossessed in the first place. And after reviewing the eight loans in question, he was right.

Sam found a stressed-looking Johnny at his desk, endeavouring to finalise the monthly repossession and auction proceeds report which must be available for Bulldog to read by the following day.

"Still going strong Johnny" Sam greeted.

"Yes Sam" Johnny sniped, "but no thanks to Workflow, who finally gave me the data I need to compile the monthly repossession report."

"I think they are under the pump," Sam said, defending Raj and his team.

"I was supposed to have it a week ago," Johnny snapped.

"How much notice do we need to give to remove a vehicle from an auction?" Sam asked

"Ideally, the sooner, the better," Johnny said, "but we can withdraw on the day of the auction."

Good," Sam said, as he placed a sheet of paper on Johnny's desk. I need these 8 vehicles to be removed from tomorrow's auction."

"Really?" Johnny replied, "does Bulld-"

"No" Sam said, "and I want to keep it that way but he will know soon which means time is of the essence."

"So you're asking me, to remove these eight vehicles from auction and do it without Bulldog, and I'm assuming Stuart and Eric, too, knowing about it?" Johnny asked.

"There is no risk to you here Johnny," Sam said, "I am taking full responsibility. As far as you are concerned, you are responding to my instructions and naturally assumed I would inform Bulldog and Stuart. The onus is on me, not you."

"I'm not so worried about that Sam" Johnny remarked, "you and I are as thick as thieves, but you know Bulldog looks at the list of cars to be auctioned regularly, it's like an addiction. He already factors in how much the arrears index will reduce before they've even been sold. It won't be easy keeping him from getting wind of it."

"That's why I want you to leave it until the day of the auction to tell Pymbles" Sam explained.

"First thing tomorrow morning, you let them know. The aim is to tell the clients they can have their cars back, with the debt waived, and they collect them on that day. The whole process will take less than 24 hours."

Bungoona Lookout, Royal National Park

Johnny digested Sam's proposal then nodded, with a wry smile as he sat back in his chair, looking a lot more relaxed. His camera, which was perched on his desk, caught his eye.

I haven't shown you my snaps from the weekend Sammy" Johnny chirped, "I spent all day Sunday and Monday at the Royal National Park in Bungoona' as he showed Sam some photos of the spectacular coastline and ocean before moving on to some native birds.

"Thanks to you Johnny, I am starting to appreciate nature more," Sam remarked. "I even sat out on the balcony with Vince the other day, the two of us soaking it up."

"That's because nature, like children, is real, it's authentic, it is what you see, and you can trust it," Johnny reacted, "unlike a certain other species, many who are more bent than a corkscrew and couldn't lie straight in bed."

"Monday as well," Sam posed, "did you take annual leave?"

"Yeah," Johnny responded, "I was reading an article recently about astrology, something I know little about, and it was really interesting. It likened astrology to photography, saying, amongst other things, they are both concerned with an ongoing attempt to capture the intangible. It maintained that the best days to take photos are Sunday and Monday because of the celestial bodies. The sun, which is from where Sunday was named, and the moon, from where Monday was named."

"What about the other days of the week?" Sam asked, "What celestial bodies were they named after?"

"They are from different gods, I think," Johnny replied, "like Thor and Thursday, that sort of thing."

"So did it work?" Sam asked, "were the photos better?"

Johnny looks admiringly at the photos and then back at Sam. "Take a wild guess."

Outside, the Corso is a hive of activity as the sun streams down on a swathe of shoppers and revellers. Ronnie and Ti have taken The Burrow stage and are preparing to perform their next song in front of a large and boisterous crowd. Over at The Staines, Bulldog, Stuart, and Eric have parked themselves at their usual table in the garden bar and into their fourth round of schooners when appearing at the front entrance is Ian Griggs.

"Griggsy," Eric yells, "fancy seeing you here," buoyed at the sight of one of his direct reports joining them.

"I was actually looking for Sam," Griggsy said as he joined Bulldog and Stuart at their table, "I thought he'd be here." Griggsy knew full well that Sam wasn't at The Staines as moments earlier he checked in on the Sensitive Matters team, from a distance so as not to be noticed, and saw Sam at his desk.

"Not here Griggsy," Bulldog said, "probably join us later. What are you drinking?"

"Nothing thanks Bulldog" Griggsy answered, "I have to get back to the team. Agents were sent to repossess a CX-9 and Sam's guys put a stop to it, so I need to get to the bottom of it. The agents have spent a lot of time and money on this one and want to get paid. But as we all know, they can't invoice us until we close the case."

"Why would Sam put a stop to it? Eric posed, "what's the scenario?"

"Deceased Estate" Griggsy explained, "debtor passed away, but the wife wants to keep the car.

The trouble is she is not on the loan and has no money to pay."

"Well, it's a no brainer" Bulldog thundered who had been listening closely, "repossess."

"The trouble is Bulldog" Griggs reasoned, "the contract is coded to Sensitive Matters, the ball is in Sam's court."

"And I overrule Sam," Bulldog asserted, "repossess."

Griggsy nodded, then quickly headed back to the office. On the way, he pulled out his phone.

"Hey Johnny" Griggsy greeted, "I need you to prepare for another car to go to auction next week, a Mazda CX-9, contract number 1-04125-01." as he stopped to check, he was quoting the right number.

Johnny brings the contract up on screen and notices the contract is coded to Sensitive Matters.

He motions to Sam to take a look.

"According to the system, it's coded to Sensitive Griggsy" Johnny said, "agents are on hold."

"Not any more," Griggsy asserted, "I've just had confirmation from Bulldog we are to proceed with the repossession, which will happen tomorrow."

Johnny ends the call and looks at Sam. "looks like Griggsy is undermining you," he said. "If this plan of yours is to work, you need to get cracking with those debt waivers."

As Griggsy resumed his walk back to the office, he could see and hear Ronnie and Ti in action.

Ti has assumed the singing and guitar duties while Ronnie is on drums as they perform Boom Crash Opera's "Dancing In The Storm."

https://www.youtube.com/watch?v=R5-BK0z4L60

Chapter 32 After All I've Done for Him

Johnny Kep completed his review of Sam's list. Some of the cars have been at Pymbles' auction yard for over a month, incurring daily storage fees. Normally these charges would be deducted from the sale price, but now that they are being withdrawn, it will be a straight cost to the client, or now Global with these debts about to be waived.

Johnny's concentration is broken by Kodachrome. "Hey Cosimo," Johnny answers, "how's my favourite mercantile agent?"

"Going OK, Johnny," Cosimo replies, "well, actually not really, you could say I have some good news and I have some bad news. The good news is, I have located the Santa Fe," Cosimo pauses.

"The bad news is" he continues, "this debtor is in all sorts of strife. Mate, she's got everything she owns crammed into her car. It would take me a week to clear the bloody thing of all her belongings before we would then be in a position to take it away."

"What is the client's name?" Johnny enquired.

"Chantelle Khouri" Cosimo replied.

Johnny knew this account. Mary had told him all about it two days earlier when instructing him to suspend all mercantile agent activity. He realised this was on his to-do list.

"Great timing Cozi" Johnny said, "I was just about to ring you regarding this. I need you to walk away. We've just been informed this client is a victim of Domestic Violence."

"Right," Cosimo acknowledged, "I suspected as much. Looks like she jam-packed the car in case the husband shows up and she has to make a run for it."

"Invoice us," Johnny instructed, "and close the file."

Johnny knew he had dodged a bullet. Fortunately, he has a very close relationship with the mercantile agents who always ring him whenever there is a shadow of doubt. While he feels it is all right to be loose with the truth with the agents, he takes a different view with his colleagues, especially those for whom he has respect. He rises from his desk and wanders over to the Sensitive Matters team, where Sam is munching on an apple, standing tall at his desk, utilising the stand-up option with Mary and Logan discussing a contract.

"I spoke to the agent regarding the Santa Fe" Johnny revealed, "and he was moments away from hooking it up to the tow truck."

"Great work Johnny" Sam praised, "Mr On-The-ball."

"Why was he hooking it up to the tow-truck?" Mary asked, "the agents were told two days ago to cease all activity."

"I stuffed up Mary," Johnny said apologetically. "I only managed to speak to them today - and that was after they rang me, not the other way around."

"You are a busy man Johnny boy," Sam said encouragingly, "whatever happened along the way is incidental. It worked out well in the end."

"Hold your horses" Mary interjected, "and thanks for sorting it out Johnny but I need to get my head around this. Are you saying that the agent found the car?"

"Yep. Incredible. These guys are the best there is" Johnny replied.

"But Chantelle Khouri is in hiding" Mary stressed, "desperate to get away from her violent ex-husband. She is not supposed to be found. We haven't even spoken to her, we are only dealing with the financial counsellor."

Bulldog, still at The Staines with Stuart and Eric, is ploughing through the schooners at a rate of knots. Griggsy's revelation has made him edgy, a plight which tends to accelerate the ale consumption. As he polishes off another Carlton draught, Renita makes a surprise appearance.

"We started early, Renita" Eric responded, "it's been a long week and we took the rare opportunity to finish a bit earlier than usual and unwind."

"Besides," Gavin interjected, "I drink to make other people more interesting," which brings a chuckle from Stuart.

"Bulldog has a way with words Renita," Stuart said.

"Has he now?" Renita reacted, "maybe he does but not with those words." Stuart looks confused.

"They're not his Stuart," Renita clarified, "they are from Ernest Hemingway."

"I never said I came up with the phrase," Bulldog chimed in.

"I sent you an e-mail Gavin," Renita said, "but I'm yet to receive a response. I thought it best I see you in person in case there was a problem."

"What e-mail?" Gavin responded indignantly, "I make it a habit of responding to everything that comes my way and I did not get anything from you."

"Look, we can talk about this in private," Renita said as she glanced at Stuart and Eric.

"It's fine, Renita" Gavin responded, "we can discuss it here. It's important to be transparent and honest."

"It was on the back of the Veteran's Voice matter and our client, Ronald Jacka I asked you to confirm when we have ceased all dealings with Scholes Mercantile, but I see in the latest batch of invoices they are still working for us."

"Oh, that e-mail," Gavin reacted, "I'm still working on it, lots to go through due to contracts, agreements, regulations, the whole shebang."

"So when can I expect an answer then Gavin?" Renita asked.

"Probably another week or so," Gavin replied.

"You have two days. If I don't have confirmation by then, I will do it myself," Renita asserted as she walked off without saying goodbye.

Over at the TAB, Sam sits alone at a table in the far corner, watching a video on YouTube of Everton's Spirit of The Blues, after Carla agreed to put it on for him, when Abbey walks in the front entrance. Carla, who is making an almond milk latte for a customer, has already been told by Sam of the planned rendezvous, and though she hasn't met Abbey, she instantly knows it is her, thanks to the numerous mentions Sam has made in their many congenial conversations.

Abbey smiles at Carla who reciprocates before looking over at Sam, who is glued to the television screen, discretely indicating to her where to go. Abbey walks barely a couple of metres when Sam notices her and immediately springs to his feet before pulling out a chair for her.

"Aren't you a sight for sore eyes?" Sam greeted "How are you, Abbey?"

"I am well, Sam," Abbey responded, "Manly sure has changed a lot."

"It just keeps getting better and better," Sam grinned as he looked at Carla, who caught his eye, suggesting it would be a good time to come over.

A new YouTube video appeared on the television screen above, "Mr Brightside" by The Killers which brings a smile to Abbey's face as she sits down at the table.

"Wow," Sam said with a hint of sarcasm, "how great is the timing? Your favourite song is playing."

Over at The Staines, Bulldog, and Stuart have left the garden bar after gusty winds forced them to retreat to the indoor section of the pub, with the only spot available being close to the jukebox, which was in full swing.

"It seems to all be happening at once," Gavin bemoaned to Stuart, "this latest push by Renita is just bizarre. I mean, where is it all coming from. The complaints have dropped markedly, so what's her problem?"

"Look, what Scholes did is not ideal, but sometimes these things have to happen to get the right outcome." Stuart said.

"You know what," Gavin remarked, "I reckon the first warning sign was those grocery vouchers, where Sam went to Renita behind my back. Then there was Griggsy's discovery of Sam calling off the agents, also without telling me."

"You think Sam might be up to something?" Stuart posed, "Surely not."

"After all I have done for him, you would think there isn't a snowball's chance in hell," Gavin said, "but I don't know, maybe he and Renita are conspiring against me."

"Don't let this get to you Bulldog" Stuart stressed, "it will soon pass over. Who is she to tell you anything. What Renita knows about Collections and mercantile agents might fill a book, but what you know would fill a library."

"Oh, don't you worry Stu" Gavin responded defiantly, "I am not giving her what she wants in two days, I will call her bluff. And Scholes are going nowhere. Renita Bray picked the wrong person to get into battle with."

As Gavin downed half a schooner in one fell swoop and slammed his empty glass on the table, a patron selected a song from the jukebox, which started to play.

"Titanium" by David Guetta and Sia
https://www.youtube.com/watch?v=KxnpFKZowcs

Chapter 33 Gone Rogue - Sensitive Matter

Friday

"He's gone rogue," Eric mutters to himself as he sits at his desk looking at his e-mail.

Eric jumped to his feet, left his bag and laptop on the desk, and sprinted to the stairs before hotfooting it to the pub. When he arrives at the beer garden, gasping and short on breath, Eric composes himself as Gavin and Stuart, each standing at their favourite table, look bewildered, if not concerned.

"I'm pretty sure he's gone rogue," Eric blurted

"Who is 'he'?" Gavin asked.

"Sam of course," Eric explained, "The CX-9 that you told Griggsy to go ahead and repossess?

He's stepped in and blocked it."

The shock of hearing this news left Gavin speechless, initially sensing the revelation couldn't be right but as he digested the news further, he realised that what Eric said was probably true.

Worse still, it looks like he wants to waive the debt." Eric added.

Stuart showed no emotion, instantly looking at Bulldog expecting an explosive reaction but Bulldog stayed silent and deadpan.

"Plus" Eric continued, "did you look at the invitation list for Sensitive Matters Friday?"

Bulldog and Stuart instantly looked at their phones and scoured their schedules. The Sensitive Matters Friday meeting had a very recent, additional invitation - Renita Bray. Gavin had a habit of rocking up to these meetings at least ten minutes late and today's affair was to be no exception but this latest revelation was enough to change his mind. Gavin looked at his watch, which showed the time to be 2.58, the meeting was scheduled for 3 o'clock.

"We'd better get going," Gavin asserted.

Inside the Skybox are Renita and Sam, waiting for Gavin, Stuart, and Eric. It's a strategic move by Sam. Not only did he invite Renita to her first-ever Sensitive Matter Friday without the others knowing, he timed it to interfere with one of Gavin's drinking sessions.

Gavin and Stuart wasted little time in getting to the meeting, walking in the skybox door at 3.01 Gavin's sartorial attire, neatly cropped hair and aroma of a fresh splash of Bleu de Chanel belied their 200 metre sprint to get there.

"I hope we're not late," Gavin says in an apologetic tone, "and hi Renita, this is a famous first, good to see you here."

"Hi guys," Sam injected, "Renita kindly agreed to interrupt her hectic schedule to join us today so I'll kick things off and maximise what time we have. The first case I'll be presenting is Chantelle Khouri."

As Sam walks to the whiteboard, which he has filled with dot points of the case, Gavin looks at Stuart as they take their respective seats around the table. He knows he has heard that name before. As he looked at the whiteboard his memory served him well. This was the case presented by Mary recently where she was seeking to waive the debt and let the client keep the car.

Twenty minutes later Sam finishes presenting the case and, unlike all previous Sensitive Matters Fridays, Gavin and Stuart are tight-lipped however, Renita is quick to respond.

"Before we talk about what to do with the loan," Renita expressed, "How are Chantelle and her three young children? Are they OK?"

"It's a great question Renita," Sam responded, and they are doing all right under the circumstances. I must say that Justice Community Legal has done an amazing job in helping Chantelle.

Aside from dealing with this car loan they assisted her with family law, child protection, and a range of other issues – and they don't charge a brass razoo for their services."

"So let me get this right Sam" Renita sought to clarify, "you are saying Chantelle's is a victim of domestic violence, she is the sole carer for her three young children, she has no assets, is effectively homeless, and her sole income is from Centrelink" to which Sam nods. "And she is still offering to pay $40 per week for the car loan?"

"Dead right" Sam said "And what is your resolution?" Renita asked, looking at Sam only.

"I think we should waive the remaining balance and let her keep the car" Sam responded.

"I agree," Renita said, "the $40 a week is far better off with Chantelle and her children than with us. What's your next case?"

Gavin was seething inside but wouldn't allow Renita to see it. Not only was he livid at a debt being waived while allowing the debtor to keep the asset, but he had been betrayed by Sam, he was a club member no more.

"OK," Sam responded, as he flipped over the whiteboard to reveal the dot points of the second matter for discussion, "the next case is Ingrid Pavlich. She has a terminal illness - cancer - four school - aged children she is paralysed from the waist down and uses a wheelchair, she had the car modified to accommodate this. She lives in country Victoria, 300 kilometres from Melbourne, and the car is the only means of transport she has to get to the hospital."

Bulldog knew the case. It was bad enough to waive a debt while the client was in possession of the vehicle but this client's car was already in the garage. What is Sam thinking of doing, giving the debtor the car back?

"Prior to contracting cancer" Sam continued, "Ingrid had been a perfect client, never missing a payment. She worked as a teacher at the local school while her husband, Altarf, was an interstate truck driver. Together they made a sizeable income and lived comfortably. When Ingrid was diagnosed she not only had to stop teaching but Altarf, who became her carer, was forced to cease employment.

'For six months they used their savings to pay bills, including the car, but when the funds were exhausted, the meagre household income was barely enough to cover essentials, which did not include the car loan."

"Good summary Sam" Renita expressed, "you certainly know your sensitive matters well."

"Thanks Renita" Sam responded, "I have a great team who keep me informed. On this one Mary gave me a thorough rundown. 'The vulnerable of the vulnerable', she always tells me, 'and they need our help."

At this point, Gavin began to fear the trajectory the meeting was heading.

"So does the arrears index," Gavin interjected. "Last payment was six months ago."

Though Gavin felt it might be unwise to express his views in front of Renita, he also thought he had to say something, believing Renita was not getting the full picture.

"I hardly think the arrears index is a consideration for this terribly vulnerable client Gavin"

Renita responded as she turned towards Sam. "What's the recovery plan for her, Sam?"

"Her recovery" Sam answered, "is for her husband to get a job, hopefully sometime soon."

""Income?" Renita posed.

"Both on Centrelink" Sam advised.

"I looked at this a few weeks ago Renita," Gavin said, "husband wasn't working then and still isn't working. The chances of either finding a job in the next 12 months are slim to none. In all honesty, the two of them haven't got a prayer."

"The husband is essentially a full-time carer, for the client and their children" Sam clarified "his wife and two children who are under 10 years of age."

As Renita sat digesting and re-reading the bullet points on the wallboard Sam waited anxiously thinking this was the loan which would either make or break his plan. While he was fairly confident Chantelle's debt would be waived, he had a few reservations about Ingrid Pavlich's situation. The balance was much higher at $45,000 and the vehicle wasn't even in the client's possession having been repossessed weeks earlier. Sam prepared himself to answer when Renita asked him for his resolution.

He didn't need to.

"Waive the debt" Renita instructed.

Before Gavin had a chance to protest, Renita rose from her chair. "Great presentation, Sam, and I'm sure you have more, but I must rush to a meeting I'm still waiting for your TAB invitation, too.

Since I mentioned a coffee and you countered with the TAB, I decided to go there for myself, first time, and it was a worthwhile experience. I recommend the Quinella. See you all" as Renita hastily left the meeting room.

An infuriated Gavin also rose from his chair, and glared at Sam before heading for the door and not saying a word. Hot on his heels was Stuart, who ignored Sam.

Sam was in a state of disbelief. He instantly rang Mary who was waiting at her desk next to Logan for the outcome of the meeting.

"It worked a treat Mary" Sam said, "Renita agreed to waive the debts of Chantelle Khouri and Ingrid Pavlich. Now you and Logan will need to get cracking. I've diverted the phone line to Johnny Kep for the next two hours. I shall see you both shortly."

Gavin and Stuart made a beeline for The Staines, arriving to find Eric and three fresh schooners awaiting. Eric had planned to attend SMW but upon learning Renita would also be there felt it would be prudent to abstain. He knew Renita and Gavin had starkly differing views and didn't want to risk appearing disloyal to either and upset his career progression apple cart.

"How'd it go?" Eric asked as Gavin and Stuart joined him at a table in the Garden Bar.

"It's official," Stuart reacted, "Sam has definitely gone rogue."

Gavin polishes off the entire schooner without taking a breath and plonks it on the table. "You realise that

Ingrid Pavlich's car was repossessed and scheduled for auction two weeks ago. The car should've already been sold."

"Sam must've convinced Johnny Kep to withdraw it from auction" Eric said.

"He certainly convinced Renita to waive the debts," Stuart said, "he painted the bleakest of pictures: domestic violence, mental illness, even threw in financial abuse-"

"Was it all true?' Eric asked.

"I doubt it" Gavin replied, "you know what these deadbeat debtors are like, every whinge imaginable to find a way to not pay."

"Is Renita aware that every time we waive a debt, we have to write ten times that amount in new loans just to break even" Stuart whined.

"I don't think she cares about that mate," Bulldog bemoaned, "too concerned for the bloody Customer."

"At least it's no longer a question, and we know for sure," Eric remarked, "Sam has gone rogue."

"I want that prick's delegation levels frozen; all authority taken from him." Gavin thundered.

"He won't be able to tie his own shoelaces without asking my permission."

Back at the Sensitive Matter domain, Logan and Mary are both on the phone, as they begin ploughing through the list of clients to contact and inform them of the debt-waiver.

"I'm not having much joy," Logan remarked to Mary, "the two calls I've made have both gone to voice mail."

"Me too," Mary said before picking up the remote control and changing the channel from the Global CEO speaking about trust to YouTube, selecting a video of Noiseworks performing "Touch."

https://www.youtube.com/watch?v=ZoHeVjVBbpM

"A change of sound to bring us a change of fortune," Mary said.

As the song plays Sam walks briskly in the door.

"How are we going team?" Sam asked

"Not much luck, Sam" Mary responded, "the clients aren't answering."

"Have you removed all the encumbrances and processed the debt waivers?" Sam asked.

"We do that after we speak to the client Sam" Logan responded.

"Sorry guys," Sam reacted, "I obviously didn't make the procedure clear. Step one is to process the debt waiver. Step two is to remove the encumbrance from the Personal Property Securities Register and step three, after steps one and two have been executed, is to contact the client."

"But what if the client doesn't want the debt waived" Logan asked, "it does happen you know where they just want to pay out the loan."

"I am supremely confident" Sam responded, "that none of these vulnerable clients will want that and if they do, we can cross that bridge when we come to it. The reason we are doing it this way is because we don't have a lot of time and I don't want Bulldog to get wind of it and stop us in our tracks."

Noiseworks' song "Touch" has reached an end on the television screen above them and a new song emerges. A picture of hands holding a human skull below a heading in Spanish, "Cuando El Amor Se Va" hits the screen before the music starts and "The Breakup Song" by The Greg Kihn Band plays.

Sam, Logan, and Mary look at each other and know they are thinking the same thing:

It is a break up all right.

https://www.youtube.com/watch?v=AffLdombeOk

Chapter 34 Debt Waivers

"How far are we into the list team?" a fired-up Sam yelled from his desk.

The two hours of Johnny Kep taking Sensitive Matters calls is almost up which means it is not only approaching 5 p.m. but the inbound lines are about to close. Mary and Logan had already agreed to stay back until as long as it takes to complete the task.

"Three to go Sam" Mary responds.

"Knock me dead if I'm a jack-in-the-box" Sam reacted "you guys are cooking like Betty Crocker. As soon as you finish the debt waivers and encumbrance removals, you can start ringing the Clients."

"I'm surprised Bulldog hasn't called you in for a meeting" Logan offered.

"Not yet" Sam responded, "but he will, that is a certainty. He was seething. I suspect he will wait until Monday morning as today he'll no doubt need to down a few therapeutic tonics with his henchmen. His ego will be badly bruised so he'll need a boost."

A loud shriek is heard across the floor. It's Mary who, while tackling the list of debts to waive has come across a name she knows very well.

"Sam!" Mary screamed, I don't believe this, Ingrid Pavlich? I thought her car was sold long Ago."

"To quote my old mate Maxwell Smart" Sam responded, "Ingrid's car missed the auction by that much" showing his index finger and thumb about an inch apart.

Whilst Ingrid Pavlich's contract was coded to Sensitive Matters, that code was removed after the vehicle was repossessed and moved to Johnny Kep's portfolio, hence why it didn't appear when Mary undertook her review of all loans to be considered for a debt waiver.

Mary goes from emotional to stunned, she can't believe it. "How did you manage to do this without Bulldog knowing because there is no way he would have agreed to it."

"You're right Mary" Sam responded "but Johnny played a key role here, the car is still at Pymbles ready for Ingrid to collect it. And yes I do agree with your inference, keeping it from Bulldog was a monumental feat, even if I say so myself."

"Of course, self-praise is no recommendation," Logan quipped before adding, "and if there was any doubt until now about your club membership, that doubt has gone long into the abyss. You are well and truly out."

"And Ingrid Pavlich is well and truly out" Mary added, "of her debt with Global. I've just completed steps one and two and all I have left now is to ring her and tell her."

"I have the last two" Logan said, "I should be finished within ten or so minutes."

Mary leapt to her feet and commandeered the Sensitive Matters whiteboard. "Is it OK if I do what I raised with you earlier Sam?" Mary asked "I think we are pretty safe now" to which Sam nodded in agreement.

When sending Sam the e-mail containing the list of loans she recommended to be waived, Mary finished the missive with a suggestion for the whiteboard. Proud of what Sensitive Matters were doing, Mary wanted everyone to know about it. Sam agreed on the condition it was executed after the bulk of the debt waivers had been processed.

Mary proceeded to write the names of each person in bold lettering and noting which of the three steps process were completed, i.e: the debt waiver has been processed on the Global systems, the encumbrance was removed from the Personal Property Securities Register and the client has been directly notified.

CLIENT STEP 1 STEP 2 STEP 3

CHANTELLE KHOURI Yes Yes No

TARA BALDWIN Yes Yes No

RONALD JACKA Yes Yes No

GEMMA CAMPBELL - Bushfires Yes Yes No

DANNY CASEY Yes Yes No

GLORIA KENNEDY Yes Yes No

INGRID PAVLICH Yes Yes No

MELISSA CARSON Yes Yes No

JARRYD BREEDEN Yes Yes No

SANDIE CHAN Yes Yes No

MARYANNE JONES Yes Yes No

REGRETS:

ALICE RHODES

AMANDA RANKIN

"And there goes the last one on the list" Logan said before sitting back on his chair, reflecting on what they have just achieved.

"Well guys" Sam said, "what are you waiting for. Get ringing."

Mary looked at the whiteboard bearing Chantelle Khouri's name at the top.

"And who better to ring first" Mary responded, "even though it won't be Chantelle who I'll be ringing but Justice Community Legal have bent over backwards to help her, as she dialled their number. "I've come up with another acronym to add to GLAM Sam and Logan" Mary chirped, AMCCAO - (pronounced am chow) All My Christmases came at once."

Logan and Sam look at each other before both responding in unison, "let's just stick with GLAM."

"And you know to whom my first call will be?" Logan posed to Sam as Mary initiated her call, "it will be Sandie Chan, thanks for approving it Sam" as he dials her number.

"Mate, you did all the work," Sam reacted, "after the case you made and the effort you put in, it was a no-brainer. A fifty-five-year-old lady who is the co-borrower for a Ford Ranger, 4 wheel drive, a vehicle she has never driven, only ever been used by her ex-partner and she herself doesn't even have a driver's license. And, critically, you got the request from her in writing."

"It's gone to voice-mail," Logan said to Sam before leaving a message, "Hi Sandie, this is Logan from Global. Would you please ring me back on 1800 041041 at your earliest convenience?"

"Who is next on your list?" Sam asked Logan "Jarryd Breeden" Logan replied, "I cannot wait to tell him the news. He's been suffering mental illness for years, minimal income but always found a way to pay this loan, incredible guy."

Sam sat back in his chair pondering what was unfolding. He looked at the whiteboard with the list of vulnerable clients, imagining their reactions when Logan and Mary inform them their debt has been waived. He pictured what is normally on the whiteboard: the team's statistics and VEW GOLF and his favourite time, Moving Day.

But then Sam thought of a different move - one where he will be escorted out of the building after being fired. Sam reasoned once Bulldog got wind of the debt waivers, all rushed through within a matter of hours, on top of his earlier actions leading to his club membership being in tatters, that this would be the last straw for Bulldog. While he was comfortable in the actions he took, Sam felt a sense of lament and disappointment that his days at Global were numbered. If Bulldog couldn't fire him for "going rogue" he would pull out all stops to make Sam's life a misery and engage in "constructive dismissal", and make the workplace so hostile and toxic that Sam would resign anyway. Sam's thoughts were for his team, about whom he cared deeply, and sensed they would not escape Bulldog's wrath. He also felt he hadn't expressed just how much he appreciated them and as he continued to gaze at the whiteboard, an idea sprang to mind.

Sam plucked his mobile phone, typed and sent a text message before leaping from his chair and scurrying out of the Global office straight to The Burrow. Sherese was tuning her trumpet, preparing to

perform solo, while Paddy was leaning back in his armchair, donned in sunglasses and a South's cap, admiring the beauty of the beach.

"Did you get my text message Paddy" Sam asked as he intruded on his relaxation.

"Yeah" Paddy responded, "and I know the song you're talking about, Dionne Warwick sang It."

"Good man," Sam responded, "only I am talking about a completely different version, the one by Rod Stewart."

"I don't know it," Paddy replied, "I mean, I know of Rod Stewart. I've just never heard him sing that song."

"Not many have," Sam said "but it's a brilliant recording and I want us to perform that in front of my team. I strongly suspect they haven't heard of either version which I'm not sure if it's a good or a bad thing."

"It's a good thing Sammy," Paddy said, "the best time to hear a song or a version of a song for the first time is not on the radio or the internet but from a live band. My only slight concern is that isn't it a bit soon to have another bonding session? You've only just done Three Nights."

"Actually my good friend, "Sam said, "it's not a bonding session, more like a farewell session, a precursor to me getting the sack."

Sherese was nearing the end of her solo effort, which was greeted with a rousing applause from the scores of onlookers who had stopped to take in her performance.

"I reckon we get Ronnie and Sherese involved too," Paddy continued, "I'll ask Sherese to bring her saxophone. We will need to rehearse though Sam."

"Of course" Sam replied, "done deal. How about later this evening, at your place, say 9 o'clock after you finish busking?"

"I'll tell you what" Paddy said "we'll finish early, see you here around 7 then we'll head to my Place."

"Perfect Paddy" Sam reacted.

Almost two hours later, in the Sensitive Matters domain, the list of clients to ring has been almost completed. Of the thirty vulnerable people, twenty-eight were contacted while the remaining two were left messages asking them to call back.

"Wow, what an effort that was" Logan uttered,

"You could say that was a wave of waives" Sam quipped, "right up your alley Logan."

"Those waives are more tiring than the ones out in the ocean," Logan said, "I am wrecked after all that."

"I am exhilarated" Mary beamed, "talk about getting the adrenaline going."

"And I am very proud" Sam said, "of you both, a superlative effort. Let's head down for a couple of celebratory drinks."

"There is every chance Bulldog will still be there, Sam," Mary said.

"I would say it's an absolute certainty Bulldog will be there Mary" Sam reacted, "but I wasn't talking about The Staines, "I have somewhere else in mind, which I am sure you will both like."

Sam, Mary and Logan packed up their laptops and made their way down the stairs. As they approached the building's exit they could hear a trumpet playing in the vicinity of The Burrow.

Sam motioned to take a peek so they headed over to find a large crowd had gathered, enthralled with percussion of Ti and the exquisite trumpeting of Sherese performing Chuck Mangione's "Feels So Good"

https://www.youtube.com/watch?v=V7dg8vRDM68

Chapter 35: GLAM

"Welcome to GLAM - where we are blessed for success."

Perched on a stool in front of a table inside the social room is Mary, wearing headphones and a broad smile. Seated in chairs about three metres away are Sam, Logan and Johnny, there to witness her trial GLAM performance. It's Saturday morning and despite the previous evening's late finish, the team is back into the office to witness Mary's proposed programme.

After consulting the IT team, Mary decided to give the idea of having her own podcast - GLAM - a go. Living at home with her parents, Mary reasoned it could be broadcast from her bedroom but before embarking on a spending spree for the equipment required, Mary wanted to test her podcast in front of a live audience. Her preference was on a day in the working week, so as not to inconvenience her colleagues, but Sam suggested Saturday, fearing Bulldog's reaction to the debt waivers on the following Monday would thwart her plans.

"The first podcast of God Looks After Me" Mary continued, "where I invite people on, from all walks of faith, to share stories of when they knew God looked after them. I, myself, have experienced dozens of GLAMs and at various stages throughout the podcast season I will share some of these, including one today, with you but the primary objective of this podcast is for you, the public, to be given the opportunity to uplift us all with your own GLAM experience.

'So, before I welcome my first guest (Sam glanced at Johnny with a look of surprise, 'she has a guest?' he muttered), I would like to kick this podcast off with a recent GLAM, very recent in fact, which happened right here at Global Bank. And a beautiful GLAM it is too.

Sam Crews, my boss, was once one of the hardest-nosed collectors in debt recovery there was.

But recently, and you could say this is a GLAM for him too, he changed. He went from an uncompromising 'cash or keys' mentality, to using his authority to help our vulnerable clients leading to, for some, a debt waiver whilst allowing them to keep the vehicle. Something which was unheard of.

Such as it was with Chantelle, a victim of domestic violence with whom I spoke last evening, telling her the remaining $22,000 debt on her loan was waived and she owned the car outright."

"How was she?" Sam asked. "Sorry, are we allowed to ask questions in this podcast?"

"That's a really good question Sam" Mary replied, "do I make this a live or taped broadcast.

Mmm. I'll have to think about that one but for today's purposes you, Johnny and Logan are there to observe and provide feedback later. However, in answer to your question, Chantelle couldn't stop crying. Finally, after all the abuse and terror she's had to endure, she gets to cry tears of joy."

Out of sight but within earshot a fake cough is heard, a not-too-subtle hint from Mary's first guest to get a move on.

"So" Mary said, "without further ado, a warm welcome for my first guest, talented busker and all round good guy, Ronnie Galah"

"Hang on a minute Mary" Sam interjected, "I thought this was for people of faith, Christian, Jewish, Muslim, Hindu etc. where does Ronnie fit into all this?"

"I am a Christian, me ol china," Ronnie responded as he walked in through the main door, looking virtually the same as he does when performing in The Burrow, donned in his prized Akubra hat, faded jeans, and a black t-shirt bearing the words "Give 'Em A Taste" in white before plonking himself next to Mary.

"Great to see you, Ronnie," Mary said, "and welcome to GLAM."

"It's an honour" Ronnie responded. "Thanks for the invitation."

"Without further ado" Mary said, "tell us all about your GLAM."

"Yeah, so a few years ago," Ronnie said, "when I was living and working in Rocky-"

"Rocky Balboa?" Sam cheekily interjected.

"Rockhampton me ol china" Ronnie replied.

Without hesitation, Mary took over. "Before you go into more details about your GLAM Ronnie, we are just going to take a quick break to hear from our sponsors." Her attention then turned to Sam.

""Look Sam" Mary stressed, "if you are going to keep interrupting you might be better off grabbing a Daily Double."

"Actually," Sam responded, "you have just reminded me that I need to catch up with somebody, so please excuse me for a bit, but I'll be back."

Sam found Paddy at a table in the TAB dining out on a trifecta while watching a replay of South Sydney's win over the Bulldogs in the 2014 NRL grand final on one of the television screens.

As the Rabbitohs' prop, George Burgess, crashed over the line to score a try, Sam approached.

"Greetings Paddy" Sam said, noticing the sheet music for That's What Friends Are For spread out on the table in front of him "fancy finding you here at the TAB on a Saturday morning watching The Rabbitohs" said with a hint of sarcasm.

"It'd be like you watching Everton playing at 3 o'clock in the morning" Paddy quipped.

"All set for today" Sam asked as he sat down next to Paddy.

"Sherese, Ti, Ronnie and I are. What about you?" Paddy posed.

"Mmm" Sam mumbled, "Yeah, yes I am. I had a few jitters earlier but now I'm fine, feeling very upbeat about it."

You know Sam" Paddy said, "this getting fired as you put it could be a GLAM."

"So you know about this GLAM too," Sam said, "gee whiz, Mary sure does spread the word."

"Actually, I didn't hear it from her," Paddy responded, "Ronnie told me all about it after he was a guest. Made me want to be on her podcast."

"Me too," Sherese interjected, who wandered in and sat down next to Sam, "I have some great GLAMs to share."

"As I was saying Sammy, this could be a GLAM for you to start something new, do something you love, like music" Paddy added.

Back in the social room, the trial GLAM podcast is in full swing with Ronnie revealing his GLAM experience.

"The boss didn't pay you for two months" Mary quizzed, "how did you survive?"

"Savings and stupidity" Ronnie replied. "He'd been telling us he wasn't getting paid by the builder but it turned out he was - getting paid - only he spent it on slow horses, punted it all, the bookies loved him."

"So that's when you decided enough was enough and upped and left."

"That's right" Ronnie said," I'd already sold my car and other things and the only possession I had to my name was my guitar. I made it to the Bruce Highway, bag on one shoulder and guitar on the other and I stuck out my thumb."

"You went hitchhiking," Mary observed.

"Yeah" Ronnie said, "and after about an hour of cars whizzing by, an old Holden pulls up and who do you think is behind the wheel - Paddy. He said as soon as he saw my guitar I must be all right before he told me he had just visited some family in Rocky and was heading back home - to Cairns, about a twelve-hour drive. Paddy and I got on like a house on fire and before you know it he's offered to put me up at his house, 'stay as long as you want' he said. We're in Cairns barely two days and he's hooked me up with a job, and he gave me some cash to tide me over until I got paid. That guy would give you the shirt off his back. So that is my GLAM, meeting Paddy Roach, and there are plenty more since that one."

"That is amazing Ronnie" Mary reacted, "and it's pretty clear you and Paddy are very close, like brothers."

"I love the bloke" Ronnie responded, "we're always there for each other. You know what they say, love is a four-letter word, and it's spelt T.I.M.E."

Johnny starts clapping and is joined by Logan.

"That was great guys," Johnny said.

"Yeah, really well done," Logan added.

"Sam asked me to add something to the end" Johnny remarked, "he said he mentioned it to you

Mary."

Oh yes, yes he did" Mary said, "I forgot all about that, a song which reflected the GLAM session just undertaken. Pity, I didn't prepare anything."

"I did," Johnny said as he grabbed the remote control to bring up a YouTube video on the television screen drooping from the ceiling above them, "though this is less about the guest and more about the host."

At the same time Mary received a text message from Sam telling her he wouldn't be heading back to the office but for them all to come down and see him at The Burrow.

"Sam's just texted me" Mary said, "he wants us to meet him at The Burrow."

Fifteen seconds later, onto the television screen came Temper Trap's "Sweet Disposition."

https://www.youtube.com/watch?v=jxKjOOR9sPU

Outside in The Burrow, Paddy is practising on the keyboard and has a harmonica set up on a stand in front of him to enable him to play both instruments, while Ti taps away on the drums.

Sam is strumming his guitar and Sherese, holding her saxophone, stands staring admiringly at the ocean.

Ronnie, Mary, Logan and Johnny are making their way down the Global stairs heading to The Corso when Ronnie decides to forge ahead, walking more briskly and is the first to arrive at The Burrow. As he approaches Sam smiles and hands him his guitar.

"Perfect timing me ol china" Sam said as they both smiled at each other.

Ronnie slings the guitar strap over his shoulder as Sam positions himself before his microphone stand as his team arrive. He catches a wave from Carla in the TAB entrance as he is about to launch into the day's first gig.

"Greetings team" Sam speaks into the microphone, as Logan, Mary and Johnny arrive, "I wanted to write a song about how I feel about you but Burt Bacharach and Carol Bayer Sager summed it up perfectly. It's like they both know us all well."

Sam steps back and Paddy plays the piano introduction before being joined by Ronnie on guitar, Ti on percussion and Sherese on saxophone.

Sam then looks at Logan, Mary, and Johnny, who are all standing together, and sings, with Paddy in supporting vocals, "That's What Friends Are For."

https://www.youtube.com/watch?v=fIuEwXBktpY

Angie appears among the onlookers while Carla watches on from the TAB.

Chapter 36 Gone

Sam, wearing a casual business shirt and his favourite Everton cap, sits on the outside deck of the Manly ferry as it makes its way from Circular Quay to Manly Beach, copping the occasional seaspray from the choppy waters and gusty winds. He appeared to be unaware he was getting wet, too engrossed in recounting his tenure at Global, as he gazed into the distance, a relaxed smile on his face and without a care in the world.

Sam thought of his time spent working in Collections, the cash or keys approach and the high fives in the team when news broke of a car being repossessed. While there was some regret over this mentality, he knew there were plenty of times when a repossession was justified and the best outcome.

A broader grin came over Sam's dial as his thoughts turned to Sensitive Matters, this is where his best memories of Global lay. It had been an invaluable and, eventually, rewarding experience and while he would miss the role itself, he wouldn't miss his colleagues, simply because he was committed to staying in touch. Once in Sam's team, always in Sam's team and leaving the company did not mean he was leaving the people.

Sam's daydreaming was interrupted by an alert on his mobile phone. It was a meeting invitation. Of course, he thought, Bulldog, just as he had expected. Once Gavin became aware of the mass debt waivers, Sam knew Bulldog would waste no time in orchestrating a meeting to send him on his way.

But it wasn't from Gavin, it was from Renita, scheduled for 9 a.m. in the Skybox. Sam spoke to Renita a few days earlier when she told him she wouldn't be back in the Manly office for a good three weeks so receiving a meeting invitation from her, face to face, was a bit of a shock. He then rationalised that after Bulldog learned of the debt waivers he immediately informed Renita who decided to execute the sacking herself.

Sam thought of his car, which he'd left at Paddy's house the previous day, having stayed the Saturday night there at Paddy's after a few snifters post Saturday's busking performance. It was a calculated move as there was something Sam wanted to do on this Monday morning which involved him driving. With what was about to unfold, he hypothesised he would not be needed in the office.

The ferry docked at the Manly wharf at 8.30 and Sam joined the throng of commuters heading towards The Corso before making a beeline for the TAB where he ordered a daily double. Despite being 25 minutes away from being fired there was a spring in Sam's step. He felt proud of his contribution to Global Car Loans and their clients and would leave with his head held high.

Sam waltzed into the office at 8.58 before making his way to an empty Skybox. After sitting on a chair at the far end of the table he looked at his phone and brought up YouTube before selecting his favourite tune, the Everton team song. As Spirit Of The Blues played he leant back with a broad smile, thinking of Abbey and Vincent. The door opens.

"Sorry I am late, Sam," Renita said, "and thanks for attending this meeting at such late notice," as she plonks her laptop on the table and briefcase next to it.

"Not at all Renita, no apology needed" Sam replied smiling, "because as they say, leave it until the last minute and it only takes a minute."

"What I am about to say Sam" Renita said firmly, "will not take a minute."

Meanwhile, Logan and Mary are at their desks, aware something of note is about to happen.

Sam sent them a message he would be late as he had to attend the meeting with Renita which they both concluded was due to the large number of debt waivers the previous day. Though they agreed with Sam's directives, they sensed Renita would take a different view while Bulldog would be incensed. All things considered, they sat nervously, fearful this may be Sam's last day.

The meeting with Renita was relatively short and sharp. The clock ticked 9.14, and the discussion in the roomy Skybox was almost at an end.

"So that's what's happening, Sam," Renita advised. "I know it's a lot to take in and will come as a shock."

Sam sat back in his chair, digesting Renita's revelation. His mind quickly turned to Abbey and Vincent, picturing them both smiling.

"I have to go, Renita," Sam replied

"Are you going to be OK?" Renita enquired, concerned the news was overly upsetting for Sam.

"I am fine Renita; I have never been better" Sam responded before smiling and leaving the room.

Sam initially headed straight to the stairs leading to the office's exit. He had his bag with him so there was no need to go to his desk. But then he thought he'd better say goodbye to his team so made an about turn and jogged to the Sensitive Matters domain. As he entered, he walked into the solemn stares of Mary and Logan.

"Are you gone?" Mary asked anxiously

"I'm outta here" Sam replied firmly.

Though she half-expected it, to now know Sam was fired was too much for Mary who became emotional and teary-eyed "That's just not right Sam" Mary bemoaned, "so unfair."

"Yes" Sam responded, "you're probably right but you reap what you sow and Bulldog's obstinance and steadfast refusal to change was his downfall. As Renita said, Bulldog lost the whole point of Sensitive Matters, he simply made it another arm of Collections whereas Renita and the powers that be didn't want that; it was to be a softly softly approach. The Ronald Jacka case was the beginning while the Hindsight Review cases were pretty much the last straw. They were all worried about the damage car loans could do to the Global brand."

Mary sensed she may have misread the situation. "Is Bulldog getting the sack too?" Mary queried.

"I wouldn't call it the sack, Mary" Sam responded, "more like a golden hand-shake and knowing Bulldog, he would've fought for a payout, probably got a poultice. The official line is his position was made redundant as there is a big restructure underway. Car Loans is to be drastically reduced." Sam then looked at Mary more earnestly, "what do you mean 'too?"

"Didn't you say you are out of here? You got the sack?" Mary explained.

"I'll share something with you I should've told you a long time ago, Mary," Sam asserted, "I have a son. His name is Vincent, and I love him dearly."

"I'll let you into a little secret, Sam" Mary reacted, "I know."

Sam smiled.

"I'm out of here to go to watch Vince play soccer; he's playing for his under-6 school team this morning," Sam clarified. "I'm not leaving Global, though now I'll be reporting to Renita. She's even talking about making me a senior manager."

"What did you say about Car Loans being drastically reduced?" Logan enquired.

"So, another big move is they are changing the way we lend in Car Loans" Sam responded, "reducing the loan types from 96 different lines down to 22."

"Are you saying we presently give loans on ninety-six different products?" an astounded Mary asked.

"Yeah," Sam answered with a chuckle, "I didn't know that either. This will mean we will no longer be lending on assets like trucks, caravans, farm machinery, tractors, there was even a category for tuxedos. Pretty much cars only henceforth and no more novated leases. They are also selling the dealerships side, so there will be no more funding of them. Plus, Global donated $20,000 to Veterans Voice. See you tomorrow."

"What about all the debt waivers?" Logan asked, "what did she say about them?'

"She agreed," Sam responded as he walked off before stopping and turning back to his team.

"She thinks you two did a masterful job; you're a couple of stars." Sam waved and turned to go, and as he reached the door "Enjoy the soccer!" Mary yelled, prompting Sam to stop, ponder what she said, and turn and face her.

"You know it will be my first one," Sam mused.

"First one, what?" Logan barked.

"My first game watching Vince play," Sam responded. "I've watched a thousand Everton games, all bang during sleep time in the middle of the night and early morning, and not one of his, which is on during our day; go figure. By the way, any news on your application for the DEI role?"

"I decided against going for it," Mary responded, "for now. I think I have more to offer in Sensitive Matters. DEI can come later."

Sam quickly left the building and breezed towards his car, parked at Paddy's place, which was a five-minute walk from The Corso and about 100 metres from the beach. Sam had already given Paddy the full rundown of his plans for that day, but that included his likely sacking. Sam sent him a message: "Still at Global, Bulldog is gone, see you anon."

Sam quickly reached his car and hopped in. As he drove off, the radio automatically came on, and the song A Thousand Years by Christina Perri started to play.

Sam likes this song and knows every bar, chord, and word. He listens as he drives, picturing Vincent and Abbey already there at the game. He imagines Vincent getting tackled and falling to the ground with half a dozen concerned mothers running from the sideline to check on his welfare. Sam thinks to himself if he were there, the first thing he would say to Vincent is, "Get up. Toughen up, son". He then thinks of Abbey, with her beautiful smile, always there for their son, looking after him through thick and thin.

Sam arrives at the ground and parks the car. He walks towards the game, where he can see Vincent playing, sixteen different six-year-olds all chasing the ball at once. He comes into Abbey's view who, though surprised, smiles at him. The ball then falls to Vince, who is only metres from the goal and a chance to score. However, he sees his dad, leaves the ball in his wake, and rushes to Sam, much to the chagrin of the sports teacher who was coaching the team, though when she sees Vincent jump into Sam's arms, her heart softens and she gives a wry smile.

https://www.youtube.com/watch?v=NZGHXy1IAHM

www.ingramcontent.com/pod-product-compliance
Lightning Source LLC
Chambersburg PA
CBHW061203220326
41597CB00015BA/1241